Supporting Diversity and Inclusion with Story

Supporting Diversity and Inclusion with Story

Authentic Folktales and Discussion Guides

LYN FORD AND SHERRY NORFOLK,
EDITORS

LIBRARIES
UNLIMITED®
An Imprint of ABC-CLIO, LLC
Santa Barbara, California • Denver, Colorado

Library of Congress Cataloging-in-Publication Data

Names: Ford, Lyn, 1951– editor. | Norfolk, Sherry, 1952– editor.
Title: Supporting diversity and inclusion with story : authentic folktales
  and discussion guides / Lyn Ford and Sherry Norfolk, editors.
Description: Santa Barbara, California : Libraries Unlimited, [2020] |
  Includes bibliographical references and index.
Identifiers: LCCN 2019036532 (print) | LCCN 2019036533 (ebook) |
  ISBN 9781440867071 (paperback) | ISBN 9781440867088 (ebook)
Subjects: LCSH: Storytelling. | Folklore—Study and teaching (Elementary) |
  Multicultural education.
Classification: LCC LB1042 .S88 2020 (print) | LCC LB1042 (ebook) |
  DDC 372.67/7—dc23
LC record available at https://lccn.loc.gov/2019036532
LC ebook record available at https://lccn.loc.gov/2019036533

ISBN: 978-1-4408-6707-1 (paperback)
     978-1-4408-6708-8 (ebook)

24 23 22 21 20   1 2 3 4 5

This book is also available as an eBook.

Libraries Unlimited
An Imprint of ABC-CLIO, LLC

ABC-CLIO, LLC
147 Castilian Drive
Santa Barbara, California 93117
www.abc-clio.com

This book is printed on acid-free paper ∞

Manufactured in the United States of America

To the Keepers of the Flame, who kept the stories alive throughout the centuries and who continue to breathe life into them today.

May your voices be heard.
—Sherry Norfolk

To the storytelling elders whose knowledge, wisdom, common sense, inspiration, and love transcend time.
—Lyn Ford

Contents

Foreword: Sharing the Love

Honoring Our World's Cultures through Stories

Margaret Read MacDonald

The peoples of our world tell amazing tales. For generation after generation, our values, curiosities, and delights have been passed down through our stories. These tales continue to please listeners because they speak to our human needs. Our students need to hear these tales from our human heritage.

Because our tales arrive from many cultures and many pathways, it is sometimes difficult for us to imagine how stories could or should be used with our students. In this collection, several tellers share stories from their own heritage and give us insights into the way these stories have fit into their own families and cultures. These insights help us in our use of the stories; they enable us to share the stories with our students with a deeper understanding than we often have for the stories we discover, uninterpreted, in books.

Joseph Bruchac, a member of the Nulhegan Band of the Abenaki Nation, shares the tale of how Gluskonba gentled the wild animals at their creation and gave us dog for a companion. Joseph's notes tell us about Gluskonba and suggest discussion questions for this story.

Gayle Ross, a member of the Cherokee Nation, brings us a remarkable magical story of two boys who befriend a snake, only to discover they have been nurturing a monster. Now they must choose between the frightening Thunder and the demon snake they had considered their friend. In her follow-up questions, Ross examines the moral dilemma the boys face.

Rebecca Chamberlain shares a transcription of Upper Skagit elder Vi *(taqʷšəblu)* Hilbert's story "Lifting the Sky," and helpfully shows us an earlier print version of the story. This gives us a chance to observe how a contemporary tribal elder adapts story for performance. Rebecca's commentary impresses on us the importance of treating the stories we share with respect for their origins.

The final story in the first chapter is reprinted from the works of Yankton Sioux writer Zitkala-Sa (Gertrude Simmons Bonnin), who worked to preserve the stories of her mother's people. We are given questions to help us think about the unusual, poetic language of the story, and notes on Zitkala-Sa's life.

Anne Shimojima shares the well-known Japanese tale of "The Crane Wife." In her commentary she helps us understand this story with its tragic ending, and the Japanese understanding of beauty and the impermanence of all things. Anne also connects the crane to the Japanese paper-folding tradition and the folding of 1,000 paper cranes to hope for peace.

Brenda Wong Aoki shares her dramatic version of a tragic Japanese tale of star-crossed lovers. This tale, for older listeners, could be read aloud or acted out. It has multiple possible endings, from various versions, but most would leave the audience in tears.

Nyla Fujii-Babb tells a story from her home island of Hawaii, the Big Island. The tale shows an old canoe maker treated poorly by an unkind fisherman but aided by a group of kind children. Nyla explains to us the Hawaiian tradition of hospitality, and the use of the coconut in the story.

Alton Chung shares the traditional Japanese folktale of "The Old Man Who Could Make the Trees Blossom," which he heard from his mother as a young boy, a tale she had heard from her mother. Alton expands our understanding of the story by telling us about the uses of rice and mochi in Japanese culture. He explains the importance of the cherry blossom season in Japanese thought. Alton discusses various versions of this tale of the kind and unkind man, some of which show the unkind man changing his ways.

Motoko gives us the strange tale of a poor samurai who enters a sumo contest in hopes of winning money for his pregnant wife. However, when an old woman hands him a baby to hold, he finds himself trapped under a massively heavy magical child. Motoko provides us much information about samurai and the culture of their era, along with discussion questions.

Donald Davis shares the Appalachian tale of "The Time Jack Went to Seek His Fortune," and talks about the Scots-Irish-Welsh immigrants who brought such stories to Appalachia and their own vision of "seeking fortune."

Olga Loya's "Margarita, La Cucarachita" includes lots of Spanish phases, and shows us how another language can be seamlessly incorporated into a story. Her insightful discussion questions help us think about what beauty really is.

Antonio Sacre offers us "The Tunic of a Happy Man." He helps us understand the blend of Christianity, Islam, and Judaism in Spain under the Umayyad Caliphate. And he shares how his own role as a father lends new depth to his understanding of the story.

Colombian American teller Jasmin Cardenas presents a version of "La Llorona," in which her babies are drowned accidentally, a softer depiction of the weeping lady than in many versions. She introduces the Colombian tale with a true story of her grandmother's encounter with La Llorona and includes interesting commentary on the origins of this legend.

David Gonzalez brings us "Chango and the Drum," which poses the question, "What is more powerful? The power to foretell the future, or the power to bring joy through drumming?"

Charlotte Blake Alston offers us a magical Wolof folktale, "Sukeyna's Journey." This tale of the kind and unkind girl motif includes remarkable images of a magic tree, a magical pot, and a terrifying old woman with a bed full of critters. This is an unusual version that Charlotte discovered when she was in Senegal.

Rex Ellis shares a true anecdote that his friend Raymond L. Redcross told him, about his way of dealing with an abusive police officer. He calls it "Yelling without Being Loud." Lyn Ford accompanies Rex's story with an

African American folktale about the relationship between cat and rat, "A Tale of Cat and Rat," and gives us discussion questions for the two tales.

Lyn Ford draws on her Affrilachian tradition to share stories of three races won by the smallest creatures: In "Contests: Tales of Competition and Determination," Sparrow defeats Eagle. In "The Tortoise and the Hare," Tortoise defeats Hare. And in "Turtle and Rabbit," Turtle wins the race with Rabbit. Lyn discusses the Affrilachian people and the value of using your wits and working together to succeed in a world of eagles, and gives us lead questions for exploring our own evaluation of these characters' actions.

"Anansi and the Magic Cauldron: An Ashanti Tale" by Bobby Norfolk tells the story of greedy Anansi who misuses a magic food-providing pot. Bobby shares remembrances of his own visit to Kumasi in Ghana and gives us suggestions for discussing this story.

Diane Ferlatte shares an African American folktale of "Ole Sis Goose" who unfortunately takes Fox to court and finds the judge and all on hand are also . . . foxes. She suggests ways to use this story to think about justice today.

It is important for all our students to hear stories from many cultures, the more stories the better. And it is particularly pleasing for students to hear stories passed down from their own cultural backgrounds. My daughter, Jennifer Whitman, teaches at the International School of Bangkok, where each of her students often comes from a different country. She makes a point each year of telling a story from each of the children's backgrounds. They wait expectantly for the week when the class will hear "their" story.

Take some of these tales and make them your own. You can share them with your students by reading them aloud, but for even more enjoyment try putting the book down and just *telling* them. These are all folktales. This means they have been shaped by telling and retelling through generations of tellers. They have been formed to fit exactly the human mind. This makes them VERY easy to learn and pass on! In fact, they are hard to forget. Don't worry about telling them exactly as they are given here; if you forget part, just invent and move on. Your listeners have no idea how the story is supposed to go. Whatever you tell them is accepted as the real story. Because you have already had a chance to read the commentary from our teller-authors, you will be able to share the stories with an honest caring for the tale's originating culture. But remember that tales move on. Once you start telling them, they will change a bit to fit your own style and persona. This is the folklore process . . . after all, you too are a "folk"! So, pick up a tale, share what you know of the culture with your students, and take the tale for a joyful telling!

MARGARET READ MacDONALD, MLS, MEdEc, PhD, is author of over 60 books on folklore and storytelling topics, including *Teaching with Story: Classroom Connections to Storytelling* (with Jennifer MacDonald Whitman and Nathaniel Whitman). MacDonald has taught storytelling courses for the University of Washington and for Lesley University. Since retirement from her work as children's librarian for the King County Library System, she travels widely, offering her "Playing with Story" workshops and sharing tales in over 55 countries.

Introduction

Sherry Norfolk and Lyn Ford

"Stories teach us empathy. They reveal to us ourselves in the skins of others."

—Justin Simien

Inspiration for This Book

Today's increasingly interconnected, globalized, and—conversely—fragmented world demands that we encourage students to appreciate the reality of human diversity and to recognize universally held values and beliefs. Folktales incorporated in curricular planning and presentation can lay the foundation for cultural understanding.

As emphasized in UNESCO's Convention for the Safeguarding of the Intangible Cultural Heritage (2003), "folktales play an invaluable role . . . in bringing people closer together and 'ensuring exchange and understanding among them.'"

Folktales can open windows into other cultures, transmitting a society's customs, attitudes, values, and philosophies of life. They can break down barriers; they can build acceptance.

In 1985, when the Haitian boat lift brought thousands of Haitian refugees into southern Florida, Sherry was a children's librarian with the Miami-Dade Public Library. Suddenly, the schools in northern Dade County were flooded with children who spoke "differently," dressed "differently," and acted and reacted "differently" than their fellow students.

The result was predictable: immediate resistance, distrust, and unrest in school populations. As one school official explained, "The Haitian kids are being metaphorically kicked to the bottom rung of society and stepped on to keep them in their place."

When their new building opened in 1980, the North Dade Regional Library where Sherry worked had begun storytelling outreach to local schools. By 1985, the schools had become convinced of the value of storytelling. It was no surprise when the library began to receive calls from desperate principals, counselors, media specialists, and teachers who asked if the storytellers might use the power of story to change the viewpoints of those who considered themselves "the Americans," so that they no longer saw their new classmates as "strangers" or "other."

The three children's librarian-storytellers accepted the challenge and got to work. Luckily for us, Diane Wolkstein had published her beautifully researched book, *The Magic Orange Tree and Other Haitian Folktales* (Knopf) in 1978, so the storytellers had easy access to a wonderful source of stories in a book that included important information about the traditional way these stories were told in Haiti, and their cultural significance. Each teller developed a small but mighty repertoire of Haitian tales and set forth.

In nearly all of the 25 elementary schools and 10 middle schools where the stories were told, the experiences were the same:

> *"Cric?" the storytellers always began. The "American" kids quizzically stared, and the Haitian kids lit up and whispered, "Crac!"*
>
> *The "American" kids' heads whipped around to see who had said that.*
>
> *The call was repeated: "Cric?" "Crac!" (A little louder this time.)*

Then the storyteller explained that she was going to tell stories from the island of Haiti.

> *"How many of you are from Haiti?" Hesitant hands went up.*
>
> *"Then you may know some of these stories!" Hopeful eyes, tiny nods—they might know one of the stories, and they would definitely welcome a familiar tale.*
>
> *"In Haiti, as your new friends know, storytelling is very important, and there are certain rules that must be followed. For example, a storyteller must ask permission of the audience to tell a story by asking 'Cric?' If the audience wants to hear the story, they answer, 'Crac!' So . . . 'Cric?'"*
>
> *"CRAC!"*

And the stories began. Sometimes funny, sometimes a bit scary, always fascinating, the stories captivated the entire audience, weaving an invisible but tangible web among the children.

At the conclusion of each assembly, the storytellers reminded the listeners that these stories were from Haiti, the homeland of their new classmates, and that those same children probably knew lots more stories to tell.

"Ask them!" the librarians urged, giving children a couple of minutes to locate and query a Haitian classmate. They saw lots of happy nods and delighted grins throughout the audience.

"We all know stories to tell each other," the librarian-storytellers finished. "You just learned that we all like the same kinds of stories. We get scared by the same things and excited about the same things and laugh about the same things. We're more alike than different. So, listen to each other's stories—and come to the library for more!"

Did those 45-minute performances work miracles? Maybe not. But they opened windows—just a crack—enough for acceptance and understanding to seep in. Principals and teachers reported that the tension in the schools lessened after that, and that children began to treat one another with more respect than fear. The stories went beyond opening windows through which to see and hear. They opened doors to invite children into one another's minds and hearts.

Folktales have the power to break down barriers. They have the power to nurture transformation. They have the power to encourage healing. The power is inherent in the stories, *even when they are told by people of other cultures*—but only if those tellers do their homework!

All three of those librarian-tellers were Anglo women, none of whom had ever been to Haiti or had Haitian ancestors. But all three did their homework, wanting to present the stories with respect, perception, and authenticity. They studied the rich background material provided by Wolkstein, who *had* been to Haiti to research the stories and the culture and traditions that surround them. They did their best to share the joy, cleverness, and courage of those tales.

Please note: They did not try to use a Haitian accent. They did not dress in costume. There was no attempt to pretend to be something they were not. And if they'd known a teller who could bring the tales from their cultural heritage, she or he would have been welcomed to tell.

What the librarian-storytellers did was watch the faces of the Haitian children, whose joy in hearing the familiar tales shone through. Their nods and smiles told the storytellers everything they needed to know: the stories took those children home again and encouraged other children to welcome them to their new home.

That is the education our children desperately need.

"Could a greater miracle take place than for us to look through each other's eyes for an instant?"
—Henry David Thoreau

"Learning to stand in somebody else's shoes, to see through their eyes, that's how peace begins. And it's up to you to make that happen. Empathy is a quality of character that can change the world."
—Barack Obama

Answers to Questions You May Have

What Is the Purpose of This Book?

The intent of this book is to provide upper elementary, middle school, and high school teachers and librarians with a treasury of world folktales that can help break down barriers, cultivate cultural understanding, and develop socioemotional awareness.

How and Why Did We Select These Stories and Storytellers?

As professional storytellers and authors, we are also students of world folktales, and we are deeply committed to bringing people together through story. We set about identifying a group of culturally diverse storytellers whose carefully researched tales authentically reflect the narrative traditions of their cultural heritages and lives. In addition to the tales themselves, each contributor was asked to provide commentary on the story and the culture it represents.

We worked toward a book that would be a resource for educators to recognize and develop curricular connections to the diversity of storytelling within world cultures, through the narrative voices of tellers living within the United States. We believe that the selected tellers, many of whom are experienced teaching artists, understand not only the relationship between story and the acquisition of knowledge, but also the dynamics of how these stories reflect on and apply to the current American experience. Their stories communicate and inform from our country's many cultures. In addition, the stories can nurture empathy and enhance interest in recognizing how we relate to the old stories and to one another.

With So Many Storytellers across the Country, Why Are We Seeing Only These Tellers and Not Others?

Our tellers honor and maintain the stories from their heritage, but their outlooks on life come from their unique experiences as folks born and/or living in this country. We set no limits on the book's inclusiveness except in that way—and we acknowledge that there are imbalances. We began with a culturally balanced list, but securing all the tellers was not easy—some folks have not updated contact information. Some want (need) payment that we cannot offer. Others are going through life challenges and career expansions that require most of their time and effort. And others have simply been too busy to return emails or calls. We understand—and, in turn, we request your understanding that our inclusiveness was only limited by the responses we received to our requests for stories.

Why Is the Dominant Culture Represented by Only One Story?

You'll note that Chapter Three: Voices Carried West from Europe to the Span of Two American Continents leans heavily toward Hispanic voices, although we did include one excellent Jack tale from Donald Davis.

This was a deliberate choice.

As this book was being developed, a national emergency was declared to build a wall on our southern border even though apprehensions at the U.S.–Mexico border remain near historic lows. Authorities estimate that approximately 12,000 migrant children are in U.S. custody, many separated from their parents. We felt that stories that represent the cultural heritage of these potential Americans—and that of the estimated 55 million Hispanic people in the United States, comprising over 17 percent of the population—needed to be heard.

A Final, Important Note

We are deeply grateful for the generosity of those who responded, and we have included all of their contributions. Many of the stories these tellers have provided are their signature pieces, uniquely refined and perfected over decades of work. The tellers are very generously offering access to these tales to be shared in classrooms, libraries, and "around the kitchen table." These carefully crafted stories remain the copyrighted works of the contributors themselves. They are *not* to be performed onstage without the written permissions of their contributors.

Prologue: Why Folktales?

Milbre Burch

Oral storytelling is the original immersive technology. Human beings have used it to communicate knowledge about the world around us; to make or strengthen or sever ties; to recall the lineage of our people and our position in that lineage for millennia. After all this time, our brains are hardwired for narrative. Story is the conduit through which we take in, remember, and recount our experiences and their meaning in our lives.

And every story begins with place. Why? Because, by and large, human beings grow up located within concentric circles of place and culture. Our bodies are the first landscape that we know, and the landscape is usually encircled by family (or what stands in for it); by neighbors and community members in urban, suburban, or rural environs; by state, region, nation, the world. Our location in those concentric circles shapes the stories we hear and, thus, our lives and our vision of what life should or could be.

The stories we are told throughout our lives are meant to teach us how to be human within the parameters of the place and culture of our birth. These lessons concern not only how to "behave" in acceptable ways, but also how to survive in a sometimes hostile environment. In time, we may hunger for other narratives than the ones we have heard or lived, and it's up to us to seek out those chronicles for ourselves. The world is full of stories that can expand our experience, our perspective, and our vision of what's possible.

Many of the narrative truths we are exposed to or seek for ourselves can be found in folktales told orally (or read aloud) from one generation to the next around the globe. Folktales take many shapes: myths, legends, fables, and fairy tales or wonder tales. These stories from the oral tradition speak to us in metaphor, inviting us to dream alongside the story's protagonist. In doing so, we venture into an imaginal realm in search of the wealth of knowledge that awaits us beyond the limitations of a single lifetime or a single point of view. That shared dream—sometimes called the story-listening trance—unfolds between the teller's lips and the listeners' ears.

When the story has ended, the listeners return from the story realm to the present day. At that moment of return, we are often changed, just as the protagonist has been, by the problems that needed solving, the challenges faced, and the joys and sorrows encountered within the story. The imagined story—along with every other narrative we encounter that has moved us in some way—is stored in the same part of our brain that stores our own lived experience. Thus, we can call up any of those tales when we are considering what consequences might result from the choices we make in life.

If you read or hear enough folktales, you know that they don't always respect regional, national, or cultural boundaries, but travel freely across them. As a folktale moves from mouth to ear to mouth or as it crosses borders, it may change its clothes or its setting or even the perspective—including the gender—of its protagonist. Why? Because no two people tell a story the same way and no two people hear a story the same way. The only time a folktale stays the same is when someone puts it in a book, closes the book, and places it on a shelf. But as soon as the book is opened, and a new pair of eyes reads it, or a new pair of lips tells it, the story begins to evolve again.

For every story that is *told aloud,* many different stories are *heard* by individual members of the audience. The tale we remember hearing is the one we were ready to hear—or need to hear—at any given juncture or developmental moment in our lives. That's why folktales appeal to everyone from preschools to elder hostels and every age in between. They speak to us about what it means to be human—even if the characters in the stories are animals and insects!

The first folktale I ever told in performance was adapted from Verna Aardema's picture book, *Why Mosquitoes Buzz in People's Ears: A West African Tale* (New York: Dial Books, 1975). A story about the large consequences of a small action, the folktale has much wisdom to offer, should we lose sight of the impact of our individual behavior on the lives around us. It was offered to me by a librarian who thought I might want to share it with the children in the low-country communities where I was working as a teaching artist. Many of those children were descendants of enslaved Africans forcibly brought to coastal South Carolina from the rice coast of West Africa.

She was right, that story was my door into a world of stories beyond the fairy tales I had grown up hearing. As an educator and an artist, my job is to offer my audiences glimpses of that wider world of narratives that strive to teach us how to be human. In my 40 years of experience, people of all ages have much to learn by listening to and sharing stories from as many perspectives as possible.

Welcome to a world of stories from the unique perspectives of some of our most talented storytellers.

MILBRE BURCH is a folklorist, a nationally known storyteller, a Grammy-nominated spoken word artist, a produced and published playwright, and an independent scholar. She has been the performance review editor for *Storytelling, Self, Society: An Interdisciplinary Journal of Storytelling Studies* (2009–2012), the co-convener of the Storytelling Section of the American Folklore Society (2012–2016), and the senior convener for the Playwriting Symposium of the Mid-America Theatre Conference (2017). She was a finalist in the National Ten-Minute Play Festival of the Kennedy Center American College Theatre Festival (2013), and was nominated for a Grammy for Spoken Word for her album, *Making the Heart Whole*

Again: Stories for a Wounded World (2007). In the United States and abroad, she has performed research on the Muslim travel ban, the fluidity of gender identity, and domestic violence. Her archival collection, the Storytelling Project, is housed in the Cotsen Children's Library, a special collection at Princeton University.

1

Voices Lifting Up the Legacy of the First Nations

Gluskonba and the Animals: A Traditional Abenaki Story

Retold by Joseph Bruchac

Long, long ago, many of the animals were larger than they are today. We know this to be true. Their giant bones have been found buried in the earth. This story, one of the oldest our people know, happened in that time.

It was the time before the human beings came to live on this land. Back then, though, there was one whose name was Gluskonba. He was the first to walk this land in the shape of a human being. He had shaped himself from the dust of creation that fell from the hands of the Great Mystery after making the earth. As a result, Gluskonba had great power. He had the ability to change things.

"Use your power wisely," the Great Mystery told him. "Use it to make things better. Soon the human beings will be here, you must do what you can to help them."

The human beings would soon arrive. Gluskonba began to think about that. Some of those giant animals that walked the earth in those days could be very dangerous. He wondered what they would do to the human beings when they first saw them. Would they seek to harm them in some way?

"I had better call the animals together and ask them," Gluskonba said to himself.

So he did just that. He called all of the animals to a great council meeting. "My friends," he said to them, "soon there will be new ones called human beings arriving here. I want to know what you will do when you meet them for the first time. Each of you, come up and tell me."

The first to step forward was Ktsi Awasos. Great Bear. He was huge in those days. He was 10 times as large as the largest grizzly bear today. The biggest grizzly bear would look like a little mouse next to Great Bear.

"What will you do when you see a human being for the first time?" Gluskonba asked Great Bear.

"ROWWRRR!" Great Bear roared, "When I see a human being for the first time, I will swallow him whole.

Gluskonba thought to himself, I do not believe that human beings will enjoy being swallowed by bears. I must do something.

So he said to Great Bear, "I see you have some burrs stuck in your fur. Come sit down in front of me. Let me comb those burrs out with my fingers."

Bear came up and sat down. Then Gluskonba began to run his hands along Bear's back. He combed out all of the burrs. Something else happened, too. Each time Gluskonba ran his hand along the back of the bear, he used his power to change things. He made the bear smaller and smaller.

"Now, what will you do when you see a human being?" Gluskonba asked when he was done.

Bear looked at himself. "Hunh," he said. "I will run away."

And that is what bears do to this day when they see a human. Usually, the only time they do not run away from humans is when they think they must protect their cubs.

The next one to come forward was a Ktsi Mos, Great Moose. The earth shook under his hooves as he walked forward. His antlers were sharp as spears and longer than tall pine trees. His hooves were huge. They were bigger than giant round boulders.

"What will you do when you see human beings for the first time?" Gluskonba asked.

"AH-HURRRN," Moose bellowed! "I will spear them with my horns. I will toss them over the trees. Then I will stomp on them until they are flat as your hand."

Hmmm, Gluskonba said to himself as he looked at his hand, I do not think that human beings will get much joy out of being speared and flattened by Moose.

So he held up his hands. "My friend Ktsi Mos," he said, "you look to be very strong. Let us have a contest. Lean into my hands and try to push me backward."

So Great Moose did just that. He leaned his antlers into one of Gluskonba's hands. He leaned his nose into the other. He began to push and push and push. But Gluskonba did not move. Instead, as Gluskonba used his power to change things, the horns of Moose became smaller and flatter. Moose began to shrink until he became the size that he is today. And his nose got all smooshed in.

"What will you do now when you see a human being?" Gluskonba asked.

Moose looked at himself. "Ah-hurrn, I will run away," he said. And so moose does even now when it sees a human—unless its calves are threatened.

The next giant animal to come forward was the one that all the other animals feared. He was the most dangerous animal. He was the most vicious animal. He was the most powerful animal. He was the one called Ktsi Mikwe.

He snarled and growled as he stepped forward and looked very frightening.

Who was this terrible animal? What giant creature was Ktsi Mikwe? It was the violent, mean, terrifying, dreaded . . . Great Red Squirrel. He was much bigger then.

When Gluskonba asked him what he would do, Great Red Squirrel screamed in a loud and terrible voice: "ARRRR-EEEEEE! I will destroy all the humans I see! I will tear them all to pieces! I will crush them under giant stones and trees."

Unh-hunh, Gluskonba said to himself. I do not think that human beings will be pleased about being torn apart by red squirrels.

So he said to Great Red Squirrel, "My friend, you have some burrs stuck in your fur. Let me comb them out."

Then, just as he had done with Bear, Gluskonba combed out those burrs while using his power to make Red Squirrel smaller and smaller. Because Red Squirrel was so dangerous, he did not stop until that Red Squirrel was small enough to fit into his hand. Then Red Squirrel leapt out and ran to the top of a tall tree. To this day you may see a red squirrel up there in the treetops. Although small, red squirrels still have a bad temper.

Sometimes when you walk in the woods, red squirrel will scream down at you in its terrible voice, screaming, "I will destroy you! I will destroy you!" Then red squirrel will hurl down huge acorns and big pinecones trying to crush you. But because red squirrel is now so small, it is no longer dangerous to us humans.

More and more animals came forward. Some did not need to be changed at all.

Rabbit, when asked, replied, "I will just run around in circles and be very terrified when I see a human being." It is still that way today.

Deer said, "I will run away as fast as I can and hide in the forest when I see a human." That is what deer does to this day.

Wolf said, "I will walk my way and the human beings will walk their way and we will not bother each other." And so it still is.

The Mice said, "We will sneak into their homes and eat the crumbs from their food."

Gluskonba nodded his head. "That is not such a bad thing," he said. And that is what the mice always do.

One by one, each animal came forth. However, when they saw what Gluskonba was doing, a few of those animals decided to hide from him. As a result, they were not changed. That is why some monsters remained in the world and, some say, are still here today. We have stories about them, too.

One animal that tried to hide itself went behind a big pine tree. However, that animal left its tail sticking out and Gluskonba saw it. Gluskonba crept up to that tree quietly and grabbed the animal's tail. The animal was so started that it made a great leap and managed to get away. However, its tail got stretched out and the end of that tail turned black where Gluskonba grabbed it. Because its tail was now as long as its body, it was given the name of Pihtolo, which means Long Tail. In English it is called mountain lion.

Finally, only one animal was left. That animal sat out there in the middle of the clearing wagging its tail. Yes, it was . . . dog.

"Will you do something to harm the human beings when you first see them?" Gluskonba asked.

"Nooooo!" dog said. "No, no, no, no! I have been waiting for them. I want to live. I want to play with their children. I want to help them when they go hunting. I want to live in their houses with them and share their food. I want to be their best best best friend."

Gluskonba smiled. "My friend dog," he said, "You will be a better friend to human beings than many of them deserve. So, you will always be with them. You will stay by their sides and you'll be known by the name Alomos—The One Who Walks With Us."

And, so it is to this day. Wherever the people go, Dog is always by their sides.

Commentary

Gluskonba is the culture hero of the Wabanaki peoples, the "Dawn Land" Algonquin-speaking nations of what is now known as New England.

His name might be literally translated as "the person who speaks," and is spelled variously among the different Wabanaki Nations, such as the Western Abenaki, the Penobscot, Passamaquoddy, and so on.

Given the power to change things by the Ktsi Nwaskw, the Great Mystery, many of the stories about him tell of how he defeats such monsters or dangerous beings as Aglebemu, the Giant Frog; Wuchowsen, the Wind Eagle; and others.

This particular traditional tale, which speaks of the time when giant beings roamed the earth before human beings were here, is one of the oldest of these stories. Like virtually all Native American stories, it is meant to both entertain and teach useful lessons, including aspects of the natural world and proper or improper behaviors.

There are a number of different versions of the story, some of which were collected in the early 20th century by such ethnologists as Frank Speck, who recorded a Penobscot version. Other versions still exist primarily in oral tradition—both in English and in our indigenous languages. This telling drew upon both written and Western Abenaki oral sources.

Discussion Questions

1. All Native American stories are meant to entertain *and* teach lessons. What lessons do you find taught in this story? Explain the actions or events that clearly show these lessons in the story.
2. Make connections between this ancient story and the world today—do you think the lessons are still relevant?
3. To you, which of the lessons in the story seems most important in today's world? Why is it so important?
4. Why do you think the stories were designed to entertain rather than simply teach lessons?

Photo by Eric Jenks

JOSEPH BRUCHAC, PhD, lives in the Adirondack Mountains of New York, in the house where his grandparents raised him. An enrolled member of the Nulhegan Band of the Abenaki Nation, much of his work draws on his native ancestry.

He and his sons, James and Jesse, work together in projects involving native language renewal, traditional native skills, and environmental education at their Ndakinna Education Center (www.ndakinna center.org) on their 90-acre nature preserve.

Author of over 160 books for young readers and adults, his experiences include teaching in Ghana, running a college program in a maximum-security prison, and 40 years of teaching martial arts.

A featured storyteller at numerous festivals, including the British Storytelling Festival, Clearwater, Corn Island, and the National Storytelling Festival, his *Keepers of the Earth* books (coauthored with Michael Caduto), which use traditional Native American stories to teach science, have over a million copies in print.

Why Thunder is a Friend to the Cherokees

As told by Gayle Ross

Long ago, in a Cherokee village high in the mountains, there lived two young boys. Today, you might call them cousins, for their mothers were sisters; but in the way of Cherokee clans, they were brothers. Close in age, there was a strong bond between the two as they grew, learning the skills they would need when they became men. When they were five years old, they were given their first weapons, a blowgun and darts, and the boys quickly learned how to hunt birds and small animals.

One day, as the boys were climbing down a rocky and rugged ravine, they came across a small brightly colored snake lying on a flat rock in front of a large cave. The boys were preparing to walk away from the rock, when, to their surprise, the snake spoke to them in a high, hissing voice. "Boys, you look like good hunters to me. I have not eaten in many days and I am very hungry. Would you find me some food? A bird, or perhaps a squirrel? I will always be your friend if you feed me." The boys were amazed by the words of the snake, and he did seem so small and helpless that the boys quickly agreed to help him. That very afternoon, they brought him two small birds and a squirrel before heading home to their village.

The boys continued to bring food to the snake and they saw that he was growing larger and stronger. The boys never thought to wonder why the snake could not hunt for himself as other snakes did, for every time they brought him the birds and squirrels they shot, he continued to say the same thing. "Feed me and I will be your friend." The boys were enchanted by the idea of such a friendship, and the snake became a treasured secret that they shared. They were careful never to speak about the snake when others were near, for fear that their parents would be frightened for their safety and would forbid them to go back to the cave to feed their friend.

Months passed, and the boys outgrew their blowguns and began to hunt, as the men did, with their bows and arrows. In this way, they were able to bring bigger game to the snake, and he grew larger and larger. One day when they called him and the great snake came from his cave, they saw that he had grown horns and his huge brightly colored scales struck sparks from the rock as he slithered toward them. For the first time, the boys were wary of his size, and spoke to him, saying, "Well, you are certainly enormous now. You have grown up and will no longer need us to feed you."

But the snake replied "Oh, but you are my friends, and you *will* feed me." And the boys heard a new and menacing tone in his voice.

Now, neither boy wanted to admit to the other that he was frightened by their old "friend," but by unspoken agreement, their daily hunts began to take them in other directions. Some time had passed before the boys went near that ravine again, but when they did, they were startled to hear the sound of thunderous explosions. As they listened, the blasts became smaller and fainter.

"Someone is in trouble down there," said one boy.

And his brother replied, "It is coming from where the snake lives!" So they hurriedly began climbing down the rocky ravine.

On the flat rock in front of the cave, the boys saw the snake they had been feeding. He had grown even larger, and in addition to his horns, he now had a great crystal embedded in his head that flashed with a blinding light. And the boys realized that their "snake" was no ordinary snake, but a great Uk'ten', the Cherokee dragon. The boys shivered as they remembered the stories they had heard about this Cherokee monster whose tales had terrified generations of Cherokee children!

The boys saw that the Uk'ten' had wrapped his coils around the form of a man and was rolling and twisting while his scales struck sparks from the rock. When the boys looked closer, they saw that the form caught in the punishing coils of the Uk'ten' was no ordinary man. It was Thunder. The boys had heard many stories about the great being who lived in the West, and often visited the land of the Cherokees in human form. The Uk'ten' had caught Thunder and was holding him so tightly that he could barely move and he could only make a low rumbling sound.

When Thunder saw the boys, he called to them. "Nephews, this Uk'ten' wrapped around me is fierce and an enemy to the Cherokee. You know he kills people. If you will shoot him in the seventh spot on his body, he will die!"

But the Uk'ten' cried, "Boys, we are friends. Kill Thunder instead! He is the true enemy! Remember how his blasts frightened you while his storms raged overhead!" And the boys stood paralyzed in fear and uncertainty as Thunder and the Uk'ten' both called to them to kill the other.

Suddenly the boys remembered what their mothers had told them when they were little and frightened by the sound of Thunder's voice. "Thunder brings the rain that makes our gardens grow. We could not live without him."

So the boys believed Thunder's words and in unison they raised their bows, took careful aim, and loosed two arrows that flew straight and true to pierce the Uk'ten' in the seventh spot on his enormous body. There was an eerie whistling sound as the Uk'ten' fell to the ground and a great cloud of thick smoke and fumes rose from his body. Thunder stepped free from the coils of the Uk'ten' and called to the boys, "Run! The fumes are poisonous and if you breathe them, you will die! Run and I will protect you!"

So the boys began to run down the valley as fast as they could. As they passed a standing dead tree, Thunder sent Lightening to strike the tree and it burst into flames. Looking back, the boys saw that the flames were holding back the fumes and they continued to run. Again and again, when the fumes came close, Lightening ignited a great fire behind the boys and the poisonous fumes grew smaller and weaker with each battle with the living fire, until, after the seventh fire, the fumes were gone from the air and a gentle rain began to fall.

Gratefully, the weary boys stopped running and stood gasping for breath, feeling the blessed rain washing over them. When they looked up, they saw Thunder walking toward them. Catching their hands in his, he pressed them on his chest over his heart. "Now we will always be friends. We will always be together, and you can always depend on me. While we live on the earth, until the world ends, we must protect and help and love one another."

As the boys walked home, they talked about all that had befallen them. They had begun by feeding what they had thought was a small helpless snake, only to discover they had been nurturing a powerful evil. They had spent a lot of time feeding him and he had nearly killed Thunder. But the boys had decided to believe Thunder. They had saved his life and he had saved theirs. And that is why Thunder is, and always will be, a friend to the Cherokee people.

Commentary

In what is often considered the seminal collection of Cherokee myths and stories, James Mooney's *Myths of the Cherokees,* collected primarily from North Carolina Cherokees and published in 1900, this beautiful story receives short shrift. Mooney included only one short version of the story where the protagonist is an adult hunter who stumbles on the fight between Thunder and the Uk'ten' and promptly kills the giant snake, saving Thunder's life. Decades later, Jack and Anna Kilpatrick, two Cherokee-speaking Cherokees, collected stories from Oklahoma Cherokees and felt this story was so beautiful and powerful that they named their resulting book *Friends of Thunder*. The Kilpatricks noted that the protagonists in this version are two young boys acting in innocence rather than an adult acting through knowledge, and their reward is the love of Thunder rather than personal power. In this, my own version, I have added some information about the ancient Cherokee clan system and how it would have affected the boys as they grew, as well as other cultural concepts. In the Cherokee cosmology, this story deals with the eternal choice between good and evil and the resulting guardianship of Thunder over the Cherokee people, a friendship that exists in a very real way among traditional Cherokees today.

Discussion Questions

1. In the ancient Cherokee world, all creatures spoke the same language so the boys were not surprised to find a talking snake. Have you ever wondered what the animals around you would say to you if they could talk? What would you say to them?

2. In this story, the boys must choose between the snake they helped to raise and a powerful being who is equally frightening in his own way. Have you ever been caught between two friends who pulled you in very different directions? How did you choose?

3. In the story, the voices of the boys' mothers helped them to see the "right" choice between good and evil. Have you ever been close to making a wrong choice of your own and been stopped by remembering the values your parents taught?

Photo by Steven Heape

GAYLE ROSS is an enrolled member of the Cherokee Nation and a direct descendant of John Ross, Principal Chief of the Cherokee during the infamous "Trail of Tears." Her grandmother told stories, and Gayle's storytelling springs from this rich Native American heritage. During the past 25 years, Gayle has become one of the best-loved and most respected storytellers to emerge from the current surge of interest in this timeless art form.

Gayle has appeared at almost every major storytelling and folk festival in the United States and Canada, as well as theaters and performance arts halls throughout the United States and Europe, often appearing with some of today's finest Native American musicians and dancers. She is in great demand as a lecture artist on college campuses and as a keynote speaker at education and humanities conferences. Most important, she continues to mesmerize children at countless schools and libraries across the country. Whether she is provoking laughter with a Trickster tale or moving her listeners to tears with a haunting myth, Gayle is truly a master of the age-old craft of storytelling.

The prestigious National Council for the Traditional Arts has included Gayle in two of their touring shows, "The Master Storyteller's Tour" and the all-Indian show, "From the Plains to the Pueblos." Internationally, acclaimed musician and composer Peter Buffett featured Gayle and her stories in his epic stage performance "500 Nations," based on the CBS miniseries produced by Kevin Costner. Gayle also produced and directed an all-native show entitled "Full Circle," which featured the Grammy award-winning Mohegan musician Bill Miller, as well as the singing and dancing of Rob Greyhill, Jennifer Meness, and the Great American Indian Dance Theater.

Gayle was invited by then Vice President Al Gore to perform at his residence for a gala entitled "A Taste of Tennessee," and she was chosen by the Clinton White House as the only Native American speaker at the giant "Millennium on the Mall" celebration in Washington, D.C. First Lady Laura Bush selected Gayle to perform at the National Book Festival's opening gala, where she shared the stage with such luminaries as *CBS News* anchor Bob Schieffer and stage and screen star Julie Andrews. Gayle's stories have opened evenings for such distinguished speakers as Maya Angelou, N. Scott Momaday, and Alice Walker, and she has appeared with such noted Native American artists as Rita Coolidge, Wes Studi, Kevin Locke, and John Trudell.

As the author of five critically acclaimed children's books, Gayle has been asked to speak at the American Library Association, the International Reading Association, and the International Board on Books for Young People. She was recently featured in the groundbreaking *American Experience* series "We Shall Remain" in the "Trail of Tears" episode. Her stories have been heard on National Public Radio on such programs as *Living on Earth* and *Mountain Stage*. From the kindergarten classroom to the college campus to the Kennedy Center, Gayle's stories have enthralled audiences of all ages. She can be contacted at gayleross81@hotmail.com.

Lifting the Sky: A Salish Star Story Told by Vi (taqʷšəblu) Hilbert

Recounted by Rebecca Chamberlain

A long time ago,
the Creator was traveling.
As he traveled, his face was shining SO brightly
nobody could see his face.

As he traveled,
he carried in his hands *many, many* languages.
And to each group he gave a very special language.
Everywhere he walked
he presented that group with a *very special* language.

He arrived at the Puget Sound area—in *my country.*
He stood and he looked around.
"This is such *beautiful, beautiful* land.
I need go *no* further.
I can stop *right here.*
Because this is the most beautiful land in the world."

And in his hands, he still carried *many, many* languages.
So now he *tossed* these languages in all directions.
Now the people didn't understand one another.
There were so many different languages.
And the Creator had left the sky too low.
Tall people were bumping their heads against the sky.
And some of them were climbing into the Sky World.
And this was not appropriate.
There was a time to go into the Sky World and not just whenever
you felt like it.

"How in the world can we fix this problem?"
the people worried.

"The Creator has left the sky too low.
And we all *don't* understand one another.
How can we fix this problem when we *don't* have a common language?"

Now wise people gathered.
And they said to the listening people,
"There is a way.
We can all learn *one* word . . . *one* word . . .
YA-HOW!
It means to proceed—to go ahead.

We could each prepare a *long, long* pole
and we could fix this problem."

"Each one of us is going to fix a *long, long* pole.
There are still trees that can be made into long, long poles.
So each one of you will help.
You know the word . . .

YA-HOW!
Now you are preparing for yourself a long pole.
And everything happens four times.
That is the magic number."

So now all the people have been gathered.
They have *all* learned this one word.
"Now you are going to put your poles to the sky.
All together . . ."

"YA-HOW!"
The sky only went up a little bit.

"Everyone has to put their backs to their poles."

"YA..A..A..HOW!"
The sky only went up a little further.

"Who is not pushing?
We have to push harder.
And maybe you all have to use a *BIG* voice."

"YA..A..A..HOW!"
It went up a little further.

"Four times.
Maybe someone is still not pushing hard enough.
This is the last time."

"YA..A..A..A..HOW!"
"OOOHHHH! We DID it!"

Because everybody worked with one heart,
with one mind,
with a common goal
you pushed the sky up where it still is today.

However
while people were doing this there were some hunters
chasing some elk and they weren't paying *any* attention
to what was going on around them.
And the elk jumped into the Sky World as the sky was being
pushed up and the hunters jumped after them.
And they got stuck up in that Sky World and they are
the Big Dipper
up there in the sky.

There also were some fishermen.
They were fishing and not paying any attention
to what was going on around them.
And as the sky was being lifted
they got *stuck* up in that Sky World and they became
the skatefish that is still up there in the Sky World.

So of course we are told
"Always be alert.
Always be alert. . . ."

Work together
and work towards a common cause
and you can do a lot with *one* word.

Note: Transcribed by Margaret Read MacDonald. From MacDonald, *Peace Tales: World Folktales to Talk About* (Atlanta: August House, 1992), 82–85.

The Changer (*dukʷibəɫ*)

Told by Chief William Shelton, Tulalip 1923

Dukʷibəɫ (the Changer) created the world. He started in the east and worked his way westward. He carried with him a great many languages, and as he created each group of people, he gave them each a language. When he came to the Puget Sound, he decided that he would go no farther, so he scattered the remaining languages here, as well as to the north and south. Since the people could not understand each other, they were not satisfied. They also didn't like that the sky was low and people and animals could go into the upper world with ease, which was not as it should be.

The wise Indians came together and held a meeting. They decided to lift the sky with sticks. One leader thought of a single word, *yəhaẁ,* meaning "to proceed," that everyone could use to lift the sky together. On the day agreed, all the people braced their poles to lift the sky. The command "yəhaẁ" was given, and they tried very hard. The sky barely budged. On the second and third try, it moved a little higher, and after the fourth attempt the sky broke loose and moved to its place today.

Just as it broke loose, four hunters that were chasing an elk, along with others, bounded into the upper world. They became constellations and stars in the night sky, such as the Big Dipper. From the time they moved into the sky, there was no more jumping into the next world, and the people were happy.

Note: Summarized by Joe Feddersen. From Vi Hilbert, *Haboo: Lushootseed Literature in English* (Seattle, WA: Lushootseed Press, 2004), 130–132.

Commentary

By Rebecca Chamberlain

"Lifting the Sky," or "The Changer," is an ancient Salish star story with a powerful message for the world today. It reveals how diverse groups, communities, and individuals can work together to solve problems and create positive change in the world. Originating from the Salish Sea and Puget Sound region of Washington State, this cosmological story is cherished by local tribal communities and storytellers. It was beloved by Vi (taqʷšəblu) Hilbert (1918–2008, Upper Skagit Tribe), who often told "Lifting the Sky" as a model for how to build unity and community among diverse peoples and languages.

Vi (taqʷšəblu) Hilbert was one of the fluent native speakers of the Lushootseed language. Her life's work involved preserving the language and storytelling traditions. Vi knew the power of stories as part of a community's lived experience. She talked about "stories as the elders' way of teaching," about Lushootseed as "the language of the land," and about "the earth as our first teacher." She knew the value of stories, such as "Lifting the Sky," to guide people during times of challenge and change. She instilled a deep respect and appreciation for the power of Lushootseed language, culture, and oral stories to pass on wisdom and knowledge essential to enrich people's lives, not only in the past, but in the present and into the future.

In learning from the stories, Vi encouraged all individuals to interpret and find meaning at their own level of understanding. In this way, the stories had the ability to inform and transform each person throughout their life. She said:

> *Our legends are like gems with many facets. They need to be read, savored, and reread from many angles. My elders never said to me, "This story carries such and such a meaning." I was expected to listen carefully and learn why the story was being told. Though guided, I was allowed the dignity of finding my own interpretation.*
> (Hilbert, Haboo: Native American Stories from Puget Sound, *ix)*

Vi included a version of the story—"The Changer," told in 1923 by Chief William Shelton (1869–1938, xʷqidəb, of the Tulalip Tribe)—in *Haboo: Lushootseed Literature in English* (130–132). She published this text of Lushootseed translations in English while teaching Lushootseed language and literature at the University of Washington in the 1970s and '80s. William Shelton's story is the basis of Vi's story, and it influenced many who learned from her. William Shelton also published a version of his popular story in 1935, and Ella Clark published another version, "Pushing up the Sky," in 1953 (148). Other versions of his story can be found online, such as "Lifting Up the Sky"—a beautiful story that includes references to birdsongs—shared by the Tulalip Tribe Lushootseed Department.

Part of a rich Salish cosmology, "Lifting the Sky" belongs to the ancient "Changer Cycles." The Changer, or *dukʷibə,* is the creative-being that changes the world from one moment into the next. These stories explore the great transformations that occur—not only on cosmological, geological, and biological scales—but also through the choices that people make in their everyday lives. Grounded in ancient knowledge and wisdom, these stories encourage people to understand, face, transform, and reflect upon momentous challenges and changes—past, present, and future. "Lifting the Sky" also references Salish star stories and constellation lore. For example, as a result of the change in the story, four elk and three hunters are catapulted into the Sky World and make the shape of the stars in the Big Dipper. Two canoes of fishermen, with a fish between them, make the shape of the stars in the belt and sword of Orion (Miller, 1997, 100–101).

The world is rich with powerful cosmological stories and traditions, and there are other stories about how the sky is lifted from different cultures. Variations on this motif include "Maui Pulls Up the Sky," a Polynesian and Hawaiian tale of how the sky is lifted. However, these stories are different from "Lifting the Sky," the Salish story from western Washington. It is important to honor and respect the integrity of the cultures and storytellers who bring these wisdom tales to us. Different cultures, tribes, and families have specific traditions about how stories and permissions are granted, shared, or used.

Vi (taqʷšəblu) Hilbert encouraged people to tell the stories so they could live vibrantly in people's lives and be passed on into the future. Storytellers and tribal communities continue to tell "Lifting the Sky," and share its important teachings. However, this is not done indiscriminately. People are advised to get proper permissions and to acknowledge the history of the story and the original storytellers. For example, in the early 1990s, at the time of the Clinton inauguration, someone called Vi and asked if they could tell "Lifting the Sky" as part of the inaugural festivities around the new administration. Vi generously gave her permission. She wanted the stories to be shared so they could be part of people's lived experience. However, she asked this storyteller for one thing: "Always acknowledge the original storytellers and the Lushootseed/Salish culture." This was Vi's cardinal request of everyone. Not to do so is considered a violation of trust and of cultural copyright.

I am sharing Vi Hilbert's version of "Lifting the Sky" to honor Vi and her important work, and to acknowledge her as my mentor and teacher. Vi thoroughly enjoyed telling the story to inspire audiences, and I imagine her happiness in knowing that the story is loved and treasured. This version of the story was transcribed and published by Margaret Read MacDonald in *Peace Tales* (82–85), and is used with Margaret's permission. In sharing Vi's story, I would also like to honor Vi's family, the Upper Skagit Tribe, and Lushootseed Research, the organization that continues Vi's work.

I am also including a summary of Chief William Shelton's story that is part of a permanent glass-art installation, "The Changer," by Joe Feddersen (Colville Tribe). This installation at the Evergreen State College in Olympia, Washington, is dedicated to Vi Hilbert and features Chief William Shelton's story. Joe Feddersen's summary of "The Changer" is included with his permission and is based on Vi Hilbert's translation of William Shelton's story *(Haboo: Lushootseed Literature in English,* 130–132). In sharing this story, I would also like to honor Chief William Shelton and his family (including his wife, Ruth Shelton, their daughter, Harriette Shelton Dover, and descendants), along with the Tulalip Tribe and Lushootseed language programs.

I share these stories and brief history in gratitude. I give thanks to the ancestors, culture-bearers, elders, and youths—past, present, and future—who embody the messages and teachings of the stories and bring them to life to encourage us as we meet the challenges in our world. I honor the legacy of the great teachers and storytellers who have passed away, and I name a few of the storytellers today: Roger Fernandes, Curtis Dupuis, Misty Kalama, Lois Henry Landgrebe, Benjamin Covington, Johnny Moses, Harvest Moon, Elaine Grinnell, Gene Tagaban, Harvey Whitford, members of Turtle Island Storytellers Network, and others. I also honor and acknowledge the many Salish tribal communities, teachers, students, native scholars, linguists, storytellers, elders, leaders, cultural-bearers, and others who are reclaiming and revitalizing Lushootseed language and stories through programs in tribal schools, communities, cultural centers, colleges and universities, and other venues. These include programs among the Tulalip, Puyallup, Upper Skagit, Nisqually, Squaxin, Muckleshoot, Suquamish, Snoqualmie, and Sauk-Suiattle; the University of Oregon Department of Linguistics and Northwest Indian Language Institute, the University of Washington, Lushootseed Research, and others.

As we tell and live with stories such as "Lifting the Sky," they remind us of the power of stories to support diversity and inclusion as we work together to create change. They teach profound lessons about human potential, integrity, and achievement in transforming challenges. They remind us of the importance of making choices, solving problems, and paying attention so we don't miss the opportunities available in each moment. Stories have the capacity to give us direction and resiliency during times of transformation and change. They remind us of our ancient connections to the earth and sky, and of the reciprocal relationships and responsibilities we have to care for the earth and one another. So, let's lift the sky. Let's work together to fix our problems. YA-HOW! Let's work with one heart, one mind, and with a common goal. YA-HOW! Let's create the change we want to see in the world. YA-HOW! Let's do it, now. YA-HOW!

Works Cited

Clark, Ella. *Indian Legends of the Pacific Northwest.* Berkley, CA: University of California Press, 1953.

Feddersen, Joe. *The Changer* (sandblasted blown glass). Evergreen State College, Olympia, WA, 2011.

Hilbert, Vi. *Haboo: Lushootseed Literature in English.* Seattle, WA: 1980. Reprinted by Lushootseed Press, 2004.

Hilbert, Vi. *Haboo: Native American Stories from Puget Sound.* Seattle, WA: University of Washington Press, 1985.

Hilbert, Vi. "Lifting the Sky." *Voices of the First People: Audio and Video Recordings from the Vi Hilbert Collection,* University of Washington Ethnomusicology Archives. http://bela.music.washington.edu/ethno/hilbert/voicesVideo.html. Accessed March 25, 2019.

MacDonald, Margaret Read. *Peace Tales: World Folktales to Talk About.* Atlanta: August House, 1992.

Miller, Dorcas. *Stars of the First People: Native American Star Myths and Constellations.* Boulder, CO: Pruett Publishing, 1997.

"sgʷəčalikʷ—Research," *Lushootseed: The Language of Puget Sound.* Tulalip Lushootseed, January 17, 2019. https://tulaliplushootseed.com/sg%CA%B7%C9%99c%CC%93alik%CA%B7-research. Accessed March 3, 2019.

Shelton, William. "Lifting Up the Sky." *Stories and Teachings,* Tulalip Tribes, https://tulaliptoday.com/about/stories-teachings/lifting-up-the-sky. Accessed March 3, 2019.

Shelton, William. *The Story of the Totem Pole or Indian Legends.* Everett, WA: N.p., 1935. Reprinted by Kessinger Legacy Reprints, 2010.

Discussion Questions

1. Compare the two story variants. What elements of the stories are the same? What differences do you discover?

2. In the Commentary, we read, "Vi Hilbert encouraged all individuals to interpret and find meaning at their own level of understanding." How do you interpret the story? What does the story mean to you?

3. The story, in both its longer version and its summary, speaks of constellations created by both humans and animals entering the sky world. One specific constellation is recognized as the Big Dipper in many cultures. Research the Big Dipper's mythologies from at least two regions or cultures of the world. Compare those stories to "Lifting the Sky." What similarities do you find?

4. Although there are many languages, the story tells us a single word prompted everyone to work together. What word, words, or phrases

are used to get people to begin a unified effort today? What words or phrases (including songs and cheers) are used to encourage teamwork?

Rebecca Chamberlain and Vi Hilbert, Upper Skagit Tribal Center, "Sharing Legends at Upper Skagit," March 25, 1985.

REBECCA CHAMBERLAIN (MA in literature, University of Washington) is a Northwest writer, storyteller, scholar, and educator. She has been teaching writing, literature, and storytelling in interdisciplinary programs at the Evergreen State College since 1996. Her publications include poetry, essays, curricula, research, and work with native elders that include biographies, studies of comparative literature, and Puget Salish (Lushootseed) language and storytelling traditions. She has taught graduate courses in storytelling and poetry for Lesley University's "Creative Arts in Learning" program (1990–2001), earth and sky sciences for Antioch University's master's in teaching program at the Muckleshoot Tribal College (2007–2008), and graduate and undergraduate courses in writing and environmental education for other universities. She has developed storytelling, interpretive, and educational programs for science, environment, culture, arts, and other organizations. She was a Washington State artist-in-residence in performance, literary, and folk arts (1987–2007), and has toured locally, nationally, and internationally as a storyteller. She practices yoga, is an avid mountaineer, a self-taught naturalist, and does astronomy field studies.

Dance in a Buffalo Skull

Retold by Zitkala-Sa

It was night upon the prairie. Overhead the stars were twinkling bright their red and yellow lights. The moon was young. A silvery thread among the stars, it soon drifted low beneath the horizon.

Upon the ground the land was pitchy black. There are night people on the plain who love the dark. Amid the black level land they meet to frolic under the stars. Then when their sharp ears hear any strange footfalls nigh they scamper away into the deep shadows of night. There they are safely hid from all dangers, they think.

Thus it was that one very black night, afar off from the edge of the level land, out of the wooded river bottom glided forth two balls of fire. They came farther and farther into the level land. They grew larger and brighter. The dark hid the body of the creature with those fiery eyes. They came on and on, just over the tops of the prairie grass. It might have been a wildcat prowling low on soft, stealthy feet. Slowly but surely the terrible eyes drew nearer and nearer to the heart of the level land.

There in a huge old buffalo skull was a gay feast and dance! Tiny little field mice were singing and dancing in a circle to the boom-boom of a wee, wee drum. They were laughing and talking among themselves while their chosen singers sang loud a merry tune.

They built a small open fire within the center of their queer dance house. The light streamed out of the buffalo skull through all the curious sockets and holes.

A light on the plain in the middle of the night was an unusual thing. But so merry were the mice they did not hear the "king, king" of sleepy birds, disturbed by the unaccustomed fire.

A pack of wolves, fearing to come nigh this night fire, stood together a little distance away, and, turning their pointed noses to the stars, howled and yelped most dismally. Even the cry of the wolves was unheeded by the mice within the lighted buffalo skull.

They were feasting and dancing; they were singing and laughing—those funny little furry fellows.

All the while across the dark from out the low river bottom came that pair of fiery eyes.

Now closer and more swift, now fiercer and glaring, the eyes moved toward the buffalo skull. All unconscious of those fearful eyes, the happy mice nibbled at dried roots and venison. The singers had started another song. The drummers beat the time, turning their heads from side to side in rhythm. In a ring around the fire hopped the mice, each bouncing hard on his two hind feet. Some carried their tails over their arms, while others trailed them proudly along.

Ah, very near are those round yellow eyes! Very low to the ground they seem to creep—creep toward the buffalo skull. All of a sudden they slide into the eye sockets of the old skull.

"Spirit of the buffalo!" squeaked a frightened mouse as he jumped out from a hole in the back part of the skull.

"A cat! a cat!" cried other mice as they scrambled out of holes both large and snug. Noiseless they ran away into the dark.

Note: Provenance of public domain: This story was selected from *Old Indian Legends* (Ginn & Company, 1901, now in public domain), retold by Zitkala-Sa.

Copies of this book have been published by the University of Nebraska Press (Lincoln: Bison Books, 1985), and several public domain book publishers listed on Amazon.

Resources

Phillips, Miriam. "Welcome to the Public Domain," *Wipo Magazine,* February 2009, www.wipo.int.

Zitkala-Sa. 1901. *Old Indian Legends.* Urbana IL: Project Gutenberg, 2018, www.gutenberg.org/ebooks/338.

"Zitkala-Sa." librivox.org/author/4267?primary_key=4267&search_category =author&search_page=1&search_form=get_results. Posted August 11, 2007.

Commentary

Much has been written by and about Zitkala-Sa. Yet it is difficult to confirm some details. For example, in five resources, I discovered different ages for her when she made her childhood departure from her mother's home, and different versions and opinions of experiences in her life. What is certain is that she lived, she wrote, she made a difference in the perceptions of indigenous cultures and the lives of many people, and she was a remarkable woman.

As you read the selected story, remember that it was written as part of a collection of tales to preserve some part of the oral tradition of Zitkala-Sa's mother's people, and to introduce its heritage and linguistic beauty to European American cultures. In her childhood, her desire for knowledge beyond the Pine Ridge Reservation alienated her from her mother's people, and her Native American heritage was used as justification for abuse by those who sought to "educate" her.

Fearing the strange red eyes, which could have been "the spirit of the buffalo" or the eyes of a cat, the mice gave up their old home. The mice left their joy, dancing and feasting, and laughing in the buffalo skull, for the darkness of the unknown. Some, perhaps all, would survive. But what would their new life be?

The ending is left to your imagination.

Sources for Commentary

aktalakota.stjo.org/site/News2?page=NewsArticle&id=8882

www.britannica.com/biography/Zitkala-Sa

Initial Citation: MSS 1704; Gertrude and Raymond Bonnin Collection; 20th-21st Century Western and Mormon Americana; L. Tom Perry Special Collections, Harold B. Lee Library, Brigham Young University.

www.kstrom.net/isk/stories/authors/bonnin.html

nativeamericanwriters.com/zitkala-sa.html

Red Bird, Red Power: The Life and Legacy of Zitkála-Šá (Norman: University of Oklahoma Press, 2016).

Discussion Questions

1. Who do you think looked through the eye sockets of the skull? On what do you base your opinion?
2. Compare Zitkala-Sa's life to the story of the little mice. What parallels do you find?

3. Zitkala-Sa's sentences and descriptive phrases are the American English language of her time. Choose a sentence that you find interesting, but archaic, and rewrite it in your own words.

4. Read aloud a part of the story. Considering Zitkala-Sa's poetic phrasings, try to reformat that portion of the story as verses and stanzas. How did reading aloud change the story for you? What proofs in the story's structure and sound influence the thought that Zitkala-Sa meant for the story to be read aloud?

5. Zitkala-Sa learned the English language of her missionary school-teachers and used it effectively in her endeavors, even though she was forced to use it and denied the opportunity to follow her family's Yankton Sioux traditions. What impact do you think her bilingual language skills had on Zitkala-Sa's progress in life, including her lectures, music, writing, and work as an activist? What impact do you think not living or speaking from her family's traditions might have had on her life as an adult?

6. What do you think are the advantages of knowing more than one language? Describe the differences in the language you speak with your peers and the language you are expected to use in school. List the languages spoken in your family, school, or neighborhood.

7. Even though she had struggled and suffered in the missionary school, Zitkala-Sa returned to continue to obtain the education she felt essential. What do you think this tells us about setting goals, making plans, and persevering?

Gertrude Simmons was her given name. She was born on February 22, 1876. She chose the name ZITKALA-SA for herself after her college years. That name translates from the Lakota language to American English as "Red Bird."

Gertrude was born in South Dakota at the Yankton Indian Agency. Her mother, Ellen Tate Iyohinwin ("Reaches for the Wind"), was a full-blooded member of the Yankton Sioux culture. But Gertrude never knew her father, a German American man named Felker, who abandoned the family. Her stepfather gave her his last name.

Gertrude lived on the Pine Ridge Reservation. But, at the age of 7, 8, or 12 (different biographies share different ages) and against her mother's wishes, she decided to follow in her older brother's footsteps and attend a Quaker "missionary school," White's Indian Manual Labor Institute in Wabash, Indiana. This school was founded by Josiah White to educate "poor children, white, colored, and Indian."

Gertrude's experiences there taught her as much as her studies. Institutionalized practices—cutting students' hair against their will, forcing them to wear shoes and keep to strict and mandatory schedules, exploitive labor practices; denying their families' faith systems to forcibly become Christians, and permitting only the use of the English language—showed her that such schools completely disregarded the cultures of native peoples.

But when Gertrude returned to the Pine Ridge Reservation, to her mother and those she had known as a child, she found that, because of her mannerisms, her way of dressing, and her education, she was alienated, made to feel isolated and out of place, by her own people.

She returned to the school, and eventually became a teacher at the Federal Indian School in Carlisle, Pennsylvania. The school's superintendent believed in the philosophy: "Kill the Indian and save the man." Of course, Zitkala-Sa left her post.

In 1899, she attended the New England Conservatory of Music in Boston and studied the violin. Eventually working with the musician William F. Hanson, she wrote the libretto and songs for the first Native American opera, *The Sun Dance Opera* (1913), based on themes from the Sioux and Ute cultural traditions. She also wrote literary works that chronicled her life and her struggles with identity, as well as books that preserved traditional Native American spoken word stories in the English language and literary format, and some narratives in her family's language.

Zitkala-Sa and Army Captain Raymond T. Bonnin (who was of Nakota Sioux mixed heritage) were married in 1902. They named their son, born in 1903, Raymond O. Bonnin, but he was called Ohiya, which means "Winning" in the Nakota dialect. The Bonnins lived and worked in Utah for many years.

The Bonnins worked in Washington, D.C. as lobbyists and activists from 1920 through 1926. In that year, Zitkala-Sa was cofounder of the National Council of American Indians. They stressed the importance of American citizenship and civil rights for Native Americans and represented various tribes at congressional hearings. Zitkala-Sa successfully pushed for an Indian Welfare Committee in Utah, and investigated the abuse of native peoples' rights, including their rights to the wealth of the oil discovered on some of their lands. Zitkala-Sa also worked for the General Federation of Women's Clubs.

Zitkala-Sa served as president of the National Congress of American Indians and continued her activism until her death from cardiac dilation and kidney disease on January 26, 1938. She was buried in Arlington National Cemetery. The gravestone says "BONNIN" on one side. On the other side, Raymond T. Bonnin, United States Army, is engraved above the simple epitaph:

His Wife, Gertrude Simmons Bonnin,
"Zitkala-Sa" of the Sioux Indians, 1876–1938.

2

Voices Coursing from the Mountains and Seas East to the Pacific Ocean and Beyond

The Crane Wife

Retold by Anne Shimojima

Long ago there lived a poor man named Yoshio. He lived all alone in the home his parents had left to him when they had died. On a cold and wintry day, Yoshio was walking down a snowy path when he looked to the side of the road and saw a large trap, and caught in the trap was a great, white crane, its feathers fluttering as it tried to break free.

"Oh, poor bird," said Yoshio. "You will die if I do not help you."

He walked over to the trap and bent down, and a man came running up.

The man said, "What are you doing? That's my bird!"

Yoshio said, "I was only trying to help it. Here, take this money. It's all I have. Sell the bird to me."

The man was satisfied, and after he left Yoshio bent over the trap again. He freed the bird and stepped back and watched as the bird rose into the sky. It circled over his head three times and flew off toward the mountains. Yoshio watched it until it was so small he could see it no more. Then he turned and went home.

Late that night he heard a knocking at his door. Who could it be so late? When he slid open the door there, to his amazement, stood a beautiful young woman, shivering with cold, for she was wearing only a thin kimono.

"Please, sir," she said. "I've lost my way. Might I come in and sit by your fire?"

Quickly, Yoshio invited her in. She stayed that night and the next three, for it snowed so hard she could not leave. But by then he did not want her to leave. She was so beautiful, so gentle, he had fallen in love with her that very first night. One day she smiled at him and said, "Yoshio, why don't we marry?"

So they became husband and wife, and Yoshio was happier than he had ever been. His formerly dark house seemed to be filled with light. But they were very poor. He had little to begin with and now there were two mouths to feed.

One day his wife came to him and said, "I see that the other wives in the village have looms with which to weave cloth. I know how to weave. I could weave for you."

Now Yoshio did have a loom in the house, for his mother had been a weaver before she had died. He set up the loom in a back room. Before his wife went into the room she said, "Now, you must promise me you will not look at me while I am weaving."

Thinking she needed to be alone to concentrate on her work, he gave his promise. She went into the room, closed the doors, and he could hear the sound of the loom—*tonkara, tonkara, tonkara, tonkara.* For one whole day and one whole night the sound of the loom never stopped. She didn't eat or sleep.

When she finally appeared the next morning, she looked pale and weak. But in her hands she carried a bolt of fabric more beautiful than anything he had ever seen. He took the cloth in his hands. It seemed to glow with a lustrous light. He lifted up one corner. It was as light and as delicate as a feather.

He took the cloth to town and sold it for a great deal of money, and they lived together well, for a while. But the winter dragged on and on. There was no work to be had. He didn't want to ask her to weave again, but one day she said, "I'll weave just one more time. But remember, you must not look at me while I am weaving."

She went into the room and this time he could hear the sound of the loom for two days and two nights. When she finally appeared she was so weak she could barely stand, but the cloth in her hands was so beautiful it took his breath away.

This time, Yoshio sold the cloth to the lord of the village, who gave him 10 gold coins. Now they lived together very well.

But only a week later the lord sent a messenger and the message was this: "You have sold me the finest cloth in all of Japan. I want another piece like it, and if you bring it to me I'll give you one hundred pieces of gold."

As the messenger spoke, Yoshio could see the gold coins dancing before his eyes. But when he told his wife, she was puzzled. "Why would anyone want that much money?"

So he said no more. But from that day, all he could think about was the gold. Whether awake or asleep, all he could see were the gold coins shimmering before his eyes. He seemed so unhappy that at last she said, "Very well. I'll weave just one more time. But this will be the last. And I beg of you, do not look at me while I am weaving."

Yoshio rubbed his hands together with anticipation and sat down to wait. *Tonkara, tonkara, tonkara, tonkara.* For three days and three nights the sound of the loom never stopped and Yoshio, sitting there, began to wonder. Why did she look so pale and weak each time she wove? How could she make such beautiful cloth when she never seemed to buy any thread? What was going on behind those doors?

The more he sat, the more he wondered, until finally he couldn't stand it anymore. He got up, forgetting his promise, walked to the doors, pushed them aside—and froze in horror, for the sight that met his eyes was not human. It was a great white crane, sitting at the loom, its chest smeared with blood, for with its beak it was pulling out its own feathers and placing them in the loom. Yoshio gave a cry and fell away from the doorway in a faint.

When he opened his eyes, there beside him was a bolt of fabric, the white cloth shining white upon white upon white, with a thread of bright crimson running through it in a pattern as delicate as tears. And he heard a voice.

"I had hoped that we could live together forever. But now that you have seen me as I truly am, I can no longer stay in the world of humans. I am the crane you rescued that day on the snowy path. I came to repay your kindness. I loved your generous heart. But now, I must leave."

Yoshio stumbled outside just in time to see a great white crane rising into the sky. It circled over his head three times and flew off toward the mountains, and Yoshio watched it until it was so small he could see it no more.

Commentary

The story of "The Crane Wife" is one of the most well-known and beloved folktales in Japan. It has influenced theater, film, opera, dance, popular music, and picture books. Its many variants include the previous story of a man marrying a woman who turns out to be the crane he has rescued, and an older childless couple who save a crane and then adopt the young girl who comes to them and reveals herself to be a crane before she leaves them.

Japanese folklore includes many stories in which a man marries a woman who then turns out to be an animal. These men marry birds, fish, clams, snakes, foxes, cats, and frogs, and these stories rarely end happily. The usual pattern is that the animal-wife leaves the man. Sometimes she has given the husband a rule that he later breaks, resulting in her departure. But actually she leaves because he has discovered her true nature, and this cannot be.

In Japanese culture, the crane, or *tsuru,* is a beloved and revered symbol of longevity and fidelity. Legend tells us that the crane lives for a thousand years, and it is a fact that cranes mate for life. There is a traditional belief that if one folds a thousand origami paper cranes, one's wish will be granted. Thus we have the custom of the *senbazuru,* the folding of a thousand paper cranes (25 strings of 40 cranes each).

One famous example is the true story of Sadako Sasaki, told in Eleanor Coerr's book *Sadako and the Thousand Paper Cranes* (Puffin Books, 2004). Sadako was a Japanese girl who was exposed to radiation as a two-year-old during the bombing of Hiroshima in 1945. She later developed leukemia and began folding paper cranes in the hope that this would grant her wish to be healed. However, she passed away at the age of 12 and has become a symbol of peace and the innocent victims of war. Today, the Children's Peace Monument stands at the Hiroshima Peace Memorial Museum in Japan with a statue of Sadako and a crane at the top. On the base are engraved the words, "This is our cry. This is our prayer. For building peace in the world."

Although Western fairy tales usually have a happy ending, it is not unusual for Japanese stories to end unhappily. On one level, "The Crane Wife" ends unhappily because the husband has broken his promise not to look at his wife while she is weaving. The consequence is that he loses her. On another level, the Japanese recognize that beauty is more complete when we accept its ephemeral nature. The concept of *mono-no-aware* ("the pathos of things") is an important idea in Japanese culture, with origins in Buddhist and Shinto beliefs. It tells us that life is fleeting and that we appreciate its beauty all the more when we open ourselves to its impermanence. One well-known example of this idea is the *sakura,* or "cherry blossom." We know that these beautiful blossoms cannot last. Because they are here for such a short time, we value and appreciate them more, and the sadness that we feel in their leaving heightens our appreciation and deepens our emotions.

Much of the power of "The Crane Wife" comes from its haunting sadness. This sorrow completes the sense of beauty. Hayao Kawai in his book *Dreams, Myths and Fairy Tales in Japan* (Daimon, 1995) tells us that beauty is more important to the Japanese aesthetic than a happy ending. This husband lost a wife he loved, and through this story we, too, feel the loss and its beauty.

Resources

Coerr, Eleanor. *Sadako and the Thousand Paper Cranes*. Prince Frederick, MD: G. P. Putnam's Sons Books for Young Readers, 2002.

De Mente, Boye Lafayette. "Mono-no-Aware." In *The Japanese Have a Word For It: The Complete Guide to Japanese Thought and Culture*, 263–264. Lincolnwood, IL: Passport Books, 1997.

Kawai, Hayao. *Dreams, Myths and Fairy Tales in Japan*. Einsiedeln, Switzerland: Daimon Verlag, 1995.

Kawai, Hayao. *The Japanese Psyche: Major Motifs in the Fairy Tales of Japan*. Dallas, TX: Spring Publications, 1996.

Kobayashi, Fumihiko. *Japanese Animal-Wife Tales; Narrating Gender Reality in Japanese Folktale Tradition*. New York: Peter Lang Publishing, Inc., 2015.

Yagawa, Sumiko. *The Crane Wife*. Translated by Katherine Paterson. New York: William Morrow and Company, 1981.

Discussion Questions

1. Why do you think that finding out the true nature of the wife was not allowed?
2. Do you think this story would be improved if it had a happy ending? Why or why not?
3. How is Yoshio different at the end of the story than at the beginning?

ANNE SHIMOJIMA, a storyteller of 30-plus years, has delighted audiences across the country in schools, libraries, festivals, gardens, museums, and senior communities, telling literary stories, folk and fairy tales, and her family's immigration story. Anne was a New Voice Teller at the National Storytelling Festival and Teller-in-Residence at the International Storytelling Center in Tennessee. Her CD of Japanese folktales, *Sakura Tales: Stories from Japan,* was released in 2017.

Anne's most personally meaningful work has been the story she created about her family's journey from Japan to the United States and through the difficult years of World War II, during which they were locked up in an incarceration camp behind barbed wire for the crime of looking like the enemy. She performs this story with photographs from her family and the National Archives, and believes that this story is especially important in our current times.

Legend of the Morning Glory

Adapted by Brenda Wong Aoki

Notes from the Writer

"Legend of Morning Glory" premiered with Maze Daiko, an all-female taiko company here in the Bay Area, with two contemporary young dancers, a jazz ensemble (contrabass, saxophone, and shakuhachi), and me performing the monodrama. My husband, Mark Izu, composed the music, and our son, Kai Kane Aoki, danced as the boy, while Ruth Asawa's granddaughter, Emma Lanier, danced as the girl. I've also performed it solo. Both ways work.

1. THE NIGHT OF THE FIREFLY FESTIVAL (approximately 10 minutes)
2. GOING BLIND (approximately 10 minutes)
3. THE STORYTELLER (approximately 10 minutes)
4. The NIGHT AT THE INN (approximately 10 minutes)
5. THE ENDINGS (approximately 10 minutes)

Scene 1: Night of the Firefly Festival

STORYTELLER. A few years ago, my family lived in Japan. Now we didn't just live anywhere, we lived at *the* most sacred place—Mt. Fuji. Mt. Fuji is older than the Japanese. And did you know that Mt. Fuji is a "lady mountain?" A goddess! *Fuji* is Ainu, the indigenous people of Japan. It's the name of their fire goddess, like her sister Pele over in Hawaii, because all mountains are one family holding hands under the sea.

Legend holds that Mt. Fuji sprung up in a single day in the shape of a fan. *(Storyteller snaps a fan open and holds it upside down so audience can see the shape of Mt. Fuji.)* And a fan to the Japanese represents the journey of life, and all these slats are the people and things that support you on your way. When you've finished *(Storyteller begins to trace the arch of the fan with her fingers and ends at wooden ending.),* you haven't really gone anywhere, you've just *changed* and that change is symbolized by the snow that sits on top of Mt. Fuji. It represents the sacred lotus, a flower that must journey through the mud in order to blossom. Every Japanese is supposed to make a journey to the top of Mt. Fuji at least once in their lives. And all along the journey are shrines to the goddess, tended by shrine maidens. Long time ago, these shrine maidens were called *Shirabyoshi.*

Before Kabuki, before Noh, before even the Bunraku puppet plays, there were the Shirabyoshi, the wandering women storytellers—who wandered the countryside telling their stories, begging alms for the goddess. I'm partial to the Shirabyoshi because I sort of fancy myself a wandering woman storyteller. This is one of those samurai stories where the girl is chasing after the guy going "Anata! Anata!" I love those! But what the heck is *anata?* Do you know it just means "you!"? But not like "hey you!" But "you" like you're the most important thing in my world, YOU! This is a story about a boy, a girl, and a promise.

(Mah moment.)

[Mah moment means actor holds and expands in stillness.]

STORYTELLER. He was fine, like poor boys can be—honeyed skin melting over muscles hard from work. Eyes kinna sad from seeing bad things, things she'd never have to see. Like his daddy going off to war and never comin' home; and his mama so broke up, she died too.

Her—now she was the boss's daughter. Spoiled, rich, and Ummm, ummm, ummh! Hair like a black waterfall fallin' to her knees.

They met on one of those hot summer nights, when it's too hot to sleep and a cool breeze feels like a silk kimono slippin' off your back. Everyone was on the river cuz it was the Night of the Firefly Festival.

(Throughout the story, the dancers represent the obsessive memory the morning glory keeps through her life's journey. Dancers and musicians enter the stage and joyously perform the Firefly Festival dance.)

Her—Now she was in a pretty boat filled with flowers, sweet wine, and giggling girlfriends *(Storyteller pantomimes the giggling girlfriends),* who caught the living fireflies and placed them in their hair, on a long finger or silken gown.

Him now—He was in a little boat hiding in the reeds. Watching, like he'd watched her ever since they were babies. To him, she was the sun. The way her eyes flashed when she was angry, the way that dimple showed up when she smiled. When you get down to it, he liked everything about her. But she might as well have been a star, so bright and far away. . . .

He knew she loved the morning glory—that flower more delicate than the cherry blossom cuz it only blooms for a few moments in the sun. She kept a fan, a memory from her mama, pure gold with a single purple morning glory painted on its face. *(Storyteller becomes the boy and recites the poem poorly but with youthful pride, explaining how the poem had been written on a tattered piece of rice paper.)*

I am the Morning Glory,
You are the Sun
I wait in the Dark for your light.

Not brilliant, no. He was her father's groom! He knew horses, not poetry! But you know how it happens. Suddenly a breeze rose up and snatched his little poem. Blew it clear across the water to where she sat with her girlfriends in their pretty boat. Then it hovered in the air like it was waiting for just the right moment to float gently down and settled in *her* lap. She looked around and saw him floating in the reeds.

(Storyteller transforms in and out of the following different characters.)

GIRL. Oh, is this haiku? Unusual structure—tanka, perhaps?

STORYTELLER. Frantically, he tried to escape but his little boat got stuck in the reeds and he lost an oar . . . The girls? They did what girls do. *(Girlfriends giggle hysterically.)* Then they pulled their pretty boat right up next to him and a big loudmouthed girl snatched his poem.

GIRLFRIENDS. Oh, Sir Poet! Sir Poet!

STORYTELLER. But she said . . .

GIRL. Stop it! Can't you see you're embarrassing him?

STORYTELLER. She snatched back the poem and jumped into *his* boat!

> Rockin' and a rollin', that little boat nearly tipped over, her laughing the whole time. *(Girl giggles.)* Then that big loud-moufed girl hollered.

LOUD-MOUFED GIRL. Oooww! Princess—you can't do that!

GIRL. Oh, hush!

LOUD-MOUFED GIRL. But—you can't do that!

GIRL. I said, hush!

LOUD-MOUFED GIRL. But he's a stable boy!

GIRL. I said hush! Go now! Go! Go!!!

STORYTELLER. The two of them watched as the girls in their pretty boat slowly rowed away.

GIRL. I saved your masterpiece.

STORYTELLER. She said, his soggy poem in her perfectly manicured fingers.

BOY. Huh!

STORYTELLER. He said, snatching it back.

GIRL, *remembering she is a princess and haughtily commanding him.* How rude! I guess I'm bothering you. You can put me a-shore right over there.

STORYTELLER. So he started to row with his one oar. Embarrassed, he rowed faster—that just made them go round and round in circles.

BOY, *furious and frustrated, he roars and rows in circles.* Rrraarrrah!!!

STORYTELLER. And now she was starting to be afraid of him, so she said . . .

GIRL. You like poetry?

BOY. I HATE poetry.

STORYTELLER. And now she regretted sending her girlfriends so very far away. So she tried her brightest smile.

GIRL, *timid and frightened.* Well, I like poetry.

BOY. Humph! *(Boy rows her in silence.)*

STORYTELLER. The current was strong and it was hard going with only one oar in the water. *(Boy continues to row.)* So she looked at him—I mean she *really looked* at him, maybe for the first time. I mean, she be knowin' him since they were babies, but tonight he looked different somehow . . . maybe it was the sweet wine. Maybe it was the way he smelled—that young-boy-almost-a-man smell. *(She sniffs the air, appreciating his scent.)* Maybe it was the way his hair had come loose and fell into those eyes. *(Suddenly she can't believe how good he looks.)*

> But whatever it was, suddenly she realized he wasn't so bad to look at at'all. *(He continues to row.)* Not at all. *Mmmm, mmmmh, MMMHHH!*

> She tried that smile again, this time fo' reals.

GIRL. Why did you write that poem?

BOY. You wouldn't understand, GIRL.

GIRL. Try me.

BOY. In my world, sometimes you gots to be *hard*. So hard I'm afraid I'm gonna break. So I write my poems.

GIRL. Was this one for me?

BOY. *embarrassed, angry, and curious.* No! But if it was, what would you say?

STORYTELLER. And they began to talk, his voice so low and rich. Hers so sweet and bright and after a while—well you know how it is . . . cuz the night was *warm* and she was *fine* and he was *juicy* and after a while their kisses tasted so good . . . they couldn't stop . . .

(Dancers enter with musicians—Dance of First Love.)

And when they did, our girl dove into the water. He dove after her and like seals they splashed in that warm dark velvet speckled with the glow of fireflies. And they thought the night would never end . . . but it did.

And they thought that there would be many more nights like this . . . but there weren't.

And they thought their love would last forever . . . well, we'll see.

(Dancers exit stage.)

(Storyteller watches dancers exit.) In the morn, they knew they were in big trouble cuz if her daddy found out . . . *umm, ummm, umm!*

But with the dawn, their love rose, big and bright reaching out to the whole world, and they realized—it was their destiny to be together forever.

And you know how we exchange rings? Well in those days they exchanged fans. Her fan was the gift from her mama, the gold one with the morning glory on it. In her most brilliant hand she wrote, "I love you forever."

His fan was simple, pure, and white. With his best effort, he wrote his poem, the one that started it all.

I am the Morning Glory
You are the Sun
I wait in the Dark for your light.

And she gave her fan to him and he gave his fan to her. And they promised to love each other forever.

But if our story ended here, you wouldn't be gettin' your money's worth. Besides you know the river of life don't flow like that—there are always twists and turns. *(Storyteller does a dance representing the twists and turns of the River of Life as musicians enter and perform the composition River of Life.)*

Scene 2: GOING BLIND

STORYTELLER, *enters as musicians exit.* For the next few years our princess spent her days turning down suitors.

GIRL, *bored and disdainful.* No. Sorry. Puh-LEASE!!!

STORYTELLER. Her daddy watched in amusement. He loved his daughter and wanted her to be happy. He was a rich and powerful lord but he knew that even he couldn't stand against the tide of their love. Besides, he had to admit he liked the boy—brave, loyal, hardworking. So he decided to help him improve his station. They were at war. There was much to do! He took the boy out of the stable. Gave him a spear and a bow. *(Boy demonstrates very poor martial arts skills.)*

Our boy fought many battles, captured much land, and brought back tons of gold. *(Boy demonstrates better and better martial arts skills.)* Soon he was the lord's right-hand man. One day he summoned up the nerve . . .

BOY. Uh . . . sir—it's about your daughter . . . I think . . . umm . . .

FATHER, *greatly alarmed.* Something happened to my daughter?!

BOY. *remembers how pretty she is, then remembers he's talking to her father.* She's fine, sir. *Fine.* I mean, fine sir!

FATHER. Then what ya tryin' to say, son?

BOY. You see sir, ever since we were little . . .

FATHER. Spit it out! Time is money!

BOY. What I meant to say, sir . . .

FATHER. Son, either say it or keep it to yourself.

BOY. I love her, sir!

FATHER. What?

BOY, *afraid now.* I love her, sir.

FATHER. What?

BOY, *with courage.* I love her.

FATHER. Do you promise to love her forever?

BOY. Yes, sir!

FATHER. Do you?

BOY. Yes, sir!

FATHER. DO YOU?!!

BOY. YES, SIR!!!

FATHER. Good lord boy, I was wondering when you were gonna ask. I'm not blind. Of course you can marry my daughter. You're somebody now, son. *Been* somebody. Time *you* started believing it. Tell ya what—let me help you out. I'm gonna give you a bunch of land, a fancy title. You're gonna be so fancy, my daughter won't recognize you. Hey! Let's keep it a secret. She'll be so surprised when she sees it's you! She's gonna be so happy! You're my wedding present, son!

STORYTELLER. So the boy was given a beautiful villa right next to the river where this story began. He was given a new name, "Lord of the River Reeds."

But meanwhile, our princess had plans of her own.

GIRL. I'll not marry some fat old man! I've promised myself to the boy who holds Mama's fan and no other. But Daddy says his greatest gift to me is this "Lord of the Weeds." He says I'll be so happy when we meet. But Lord of the Weeds/Reeds, whatever your name is, we'll never meet because I won't have you!!!

STORYTELLER. Finally, the day of the betrothal arrived. Dressed in silk threads, gold rings on his hands, his dark hair shining in the sun, our boy cut a fine figure when he went to her father's house to claim her. Hours went by . . . still he waited in the courtyard, her favorite flowers, the morning glory now wilting in his hand. Then her father appeared.

FATHER. My daughter, she's gone!!

STORYTELLER, *snaps her fan closed and holds in stillness for a Mah moment, then says the line.* She'd run away.

At first it was fun! Wearing RAGS. Pretending to be a boy. *(Swaggers around stage like a boy.)*

She went straight to her lover's house. But when she got there, she was told he didn't live there anymore. No one seemed to know where he'd gone. Someone said her father had made him a soldier and sent him far away to fight a war.

GIRL. Just to keep us apart. *(She sings "I Will Follow Him" by Peggy March.)* So I will follow him, follow him wherever he may go . . .

STORYTELLER. She was hungry so she went into her favorite teahouse and was promptly thrown out.

GIRL. Well, at least my disguise works.

STORYTELLER. So she ate from the rude food stalls that lined the busy corridors of the city. The meat was so stringy and tough she had no idea what kind of animal it was.

GIRL. How can people eat this?

STORYTELLER. She'd never been alone before. But she was not afraid *(Girl begins to limp.)* . . . Her feet ached. They had never touched the dust of the road; she had always been carried in a palanquin.

She came across a house barricaded behind a bamboo fence, guarded by soldiers. Hands big and little reaching through the slats fluttering like autumn leaves. *(Storyteller performs movement sequence with her hands.)* "Water! Water!"

SOLDIER. Move! Poxed they are. Move! Or join them.

STORYTELLER. The princess hurried on her way.

She came upon a bundle of rags, lying by the side of the road. The pile shifted, and the sunken face of a one-eyed woman emerged, a tiny baby sucking futilely at her flaccid breast.

BEGGAR. Help, me? Food for my baby. What are you staring at? You'll be stuck in the muck soon enough yourself, Ducky! *(Beggar's laughter gradually transforms into sobs.)*

STORYTELLER. The princess had never seen such poverty, and her soul recoiled even as her heart reached out. But her feet kept moving her farther and farther away from her father's house, so great was her longing for the boy . . .

One night lost in a deep forest, she saw a lone campfire. Cold, she was so very cold. She crept closer. Saw it was tended by rough-looking men. Still cold, she was, and *starving*.

She joined them, lowering her face and her eyes. Sat by the fire, warmed by their drink. But something about her gave her away—her voice maybe, maybe the way she held the cup, or maybe it was just that her luck had run out. Someone snatched off her cap. Her hair tumbled loose.

MAN. It's a girl!

GIRL. No, let me go.

MAN #2, *lewdly.* A GIRL?!!

GIRL. No! Please, let me go!!

ALL MEN. We like girls!!

GIRL. NO! NO! NOOOO!!!! *(Frantic, violent movements as the men violate her.)*

STORYTELLER. When it was *done,* she lay shuddering in the snow, weeping bitter tears trying to remember the sound of her lover's voice, the warmth of his hand holding hers, and a promise he had made. Until the hard, cold world around her drifted away and all she could see was the boy. For she had cried her eyes out and was now quite blind. *(Through the last lines she slowly, painfully rises and discovers she's now blind.)*

(Big Taiko Drum Composition.)

Scene 3: THE STORYTELLER

STORYTELLER. Well, they say that what don't kill you makes you stronger. Our girl picked herself up, washed her face, fixed her hair. Wandering the countryside, she became one of the wandering women, telling her story.

WOMAN. *(The girl is a woman now.)* They say I am blind but that's not true. I see with *(gesture to heart),* the eye that sees truly.

I see a boy who once loved a girl.

And they loved each other since love was love.

But alas, he was a poor boy. She a king's daughter so he left her to seek his fortune—to be worthy of her hand.

But before he went, he promised: *(Melody from English ballad, "Fare Thee Well.")*

Fare thee well my love, I must be gone / To leave you for a while
If I roam away, I'll come back again / If I roam 10,000 miles my dear,
If I roam 10,000 years.
I know her faith never faltered for *I am her. (Continues singing.)*
The sea will never run dry my dear
Nor the rocks ever melt with the sun
And I never will prove false to the boy I love / Till all these things
be one my dear
Till all these things be done. *(Song ends.)*

(Spoken) If you see my love, tell him I wait. I wait in the dark for his light.

    I am here, Anata. . . .

    And her legend spread, and she became known as the Morning Glory.

(Mah moment.)

Late one afternoon, she chanced upon a little inn by the side of the great River Oi, the kind innkeeper, seeing her sightless eyes and torn kimono, invited her to stay and eat.

WOMAN. But kind innkeeper, to repay your kindness, I have only a song and a prayer.

STORYTELLER. And the innkeeper said . . .

INNKEEPER. That'll do, because aren't you the one they call the Morning Glory?

WOMAN. Yes.

INNKEEPER. I'd be honored if you would sing for my guests tonight.

STORYTELLER. So that night and for many nights after, she sang for her supper and the little inn prospered. *(She sings her song without words on* Ooooh.)

    Months passed. Years passed.

    One day the innkeeper said . . . *(Everyone is decades older now. The innkeeper old, the woman aged, and the boy now an angry, lonely man.)*

INNKEEPER. My dear, from this day forward, half of what we make is yours!

WOMAN, *shaking head no.* Oh no, kind innkeeper! You've been like a father to me, saving the life of this worthless girl. It is enough that you provide me food and shelter.

INNKEEPER. But my dear, what of the future? I grow old!

WOMAN. Ah, but my love will come. He will provide.

INNKEEPER, *kindly but frustrated.* The river of life only flows the one way, my dear. Maybe he's already down the stream and the current of time is too strong for him to come back for you.

WOMAN. Oh, no. He's almost here. I can feel it.

INNKEEPER. Yes, my dear, but until he *gets* here, can't I give you a little something to save for your future?

WOMAN. But I don't need anything.

INNKEEPER. Are you sure?

WOMAN. No, nothing—well, maybe a kimono.

INNKEEPER. A kimono?

WOMAN. Yes—with the morning glory embroidered *(points to sleeves).* White for the purity of our love and silver for our faith kept even in the darkest night with only the stars to guide us. Oh! Kind innkeeper. Thank you. I *will* keep some of your money. For my kimono! It will be my wedding dress!

INNKEEPER, *astonished and disappointed at her delusion.* Your wedding dress?!

(She nods, smiling slightly crazed, and sings her sad song but in a strange, deranged key as the young lovers come in and dance a variation on the Dance of First Love.)

Scene 4: THE NIGHT AT THE INN

STORYTELLER. It was the ninth moon, the time of the Divine Wind, the kamikaze—the typhoon. Our boy was a man now, successful, *rich . . . BITTER. (Storyteller says next lines as angry older man, the boy grown up.)* All that he *was* had been for her and she had run away.

He never did find out where she had gone. Never bothered to look. It was clear enough. She'd run away. Must've found out her father was gonna marry her off to a "stable boy." Found someone else—fled.

MAN. Well, to hell with her! It wasn't enough that she had made a fool of me. But she broke her father's heart. The old man went to his grave crying her name. His princess! Hah!

STORYTELLER. So he buried his love under his work.

Time heals. Money helps. Still he kept her fan.

Late one afternoon, he chanced upon a little inn by the side of the great River Oi, swollen with the autumn tempests. The noodles were delicious, the inn clean and warm. A typhoon threatened, and the innkeeper begged him to stay.

INNKEEPER. Besides, my lord, you must listen to our storyteller. She renews one's faith in the power of love.

MAN. Hah! Love!

STORYTELLER. Nevertheless, he slid open a shoji screen and joined a large crowd soaked with sake.

(Storyteller pantomimes being a man and a woman at a tawdry sake party getting progressively drunk. Then opens up a sliding screen and becomes the Morning Glory.)

Suddenly a painted screen slid open and a woman entered the room. Her long hair, burnished with silver, fell like a waterfall to her knees. Her handsome face etched with the lines of a hard life survived. Then he noticed she was blind . . . the room grew quiet. She was about to begin her performance but she hesitated and seemed to look right at him.

WOMAN. They say I am blind but I see with *(gesture to heart)* the eye that sees truly. I see a boy who once loved this girl—and they loved each other since love was love . . .

STORYTELLER. And the woman opened a fan, simple, pure, white, and with her fingers traced the words.

WOMAN. I am the Morning Glory, you are the Sun . . .

STORYTELLER. The man froze. He recognized that fan. It was *his* fan. But that woman, why did *she* have it? Slowly the years faded away, and layers of war, work, and loneliness lifted and he could see. It was her!

MAN. Drunk, I must be drunk! Air! I need air!

STORYTELLER. He knocked over the table. Stumbled out of the room and bumped into the innkeeper.

INNKEEPER. My lord, what's wrong?!

MAN (BOY grown up), *shaken*. That woman! Who is she? That storyteller!

INNKEEPER. Our princess? It's such a sad tale. She couldn't marry the man her father had chosen because she had vowed to marry another. So she ran away and sought this lover up and down the country, weeping until she *went blind*. Trying to make it easy for him to find her, she sings that sad tale.

      The FIEND! I'm sure he never even looked. All these years, she's kept her faith in that phantom lover, eking out an existence as a storyteller. Every penny I pay her goes to her "wedding dress" *(trembling in anger)*.

MAN. Wedding dress?!!

INNKEEPER. She's still waiting for him! The fan she holds is *his* fan—a relic from that cruel, cruel lover.

MAN. No! It can't be true!

INNKEEPER. It is true!! He doesn't deserve to live!

MAN. Please, stop! I can't bear it!

INNKEEPER. Neither can I!

STORYTELLER. But the man looked like he had seen a ghost.

      The blood drained from his face and he crumpled to the ground.

INNKEEPER. My lord! Are you all right?

STORYTELLER. With a trembling hand, the man reached into the folds of his kimono and pulled out a silk purse.

MAN. Please see that she never wants for anything.

INNKEEPER. But . . . but . . . Who do I say it's from?

MAN. Ask her, if she remembers the Night of the Firefly Festival. Tell her it's from the boy who promised to love her forever.

INNKEEPER, *hard of hearing*. Pardon me, sir? Who?

MAN. Tell her the boy from the Firefly Festival . . . is me, the Lord of the River Reeds. . . . Give her this. *(He hands the innkeeper her fan and sobs.)* Tell her I'm sorry!

STORYTELLER. And he disappeared into the stormy night just as the Morning Glory emerged.

INNKEEPER. My dear! You are rich!

STORYTELLER. And he gave her the silk purse.

WOMAN. But who is it from?

INNKEEPER. The man said he was the Lord of the River Reeds.

WOMAN. I remember the Lord of the River Reeds. He wanted to marry me when I was a girl. He must be very old by now.

INNKEEPER. No—he was about your age. Very well-to-do. And very moved by your performance. He also said to give you this . . . *(He hands her the fan and she opens it.)*

WOMAN, *traces the writing on the fan with her fingers and gasps.* . . . Is it? No, don't tell me. It's gold with a single morning glory.

INNKEEPER, *surprised she seems to read it.* Yes . . .

WOMAN. The Lord of the River Reeds?

INNKEEPER. Yes, he said to tell you he used to give you fireflies when he was a boy . . .

WOMAN. Firefly boy? Lord of the River Reeds?

INNKEEPER. That's it! He said to tell you the boy from the fireflies is the Lord of the River Reeds and he's very, very sorry! *(He waits, proud of himself, anticipating her joy.)*

WOMAN. The Lord of the River Reeds is the boy from the Firefly Festival?!! My father's greatest gift to me!! . . . Oh, no! . . . All these years? . . . These wasted years! *(She begins to sob, tracing the fan with her fingers, reading aloud and crying.)* I love you forever . . .

> *(Thinking her lover has come for her, she tries to fix her hair.)* Oh! Silly me! . . . He's here now . . . and we can go home to my father. I will wear my wedding dress and everything. Everything will be as it was! *(She wipes her tears and straightens her clothes.)*

> Where is he?

INNKEEPER, *afraid to speak, almost in a whisper.* He's . . . gone . . .

WOMAN. Noooo! Nooo!

STORYTELLER. . . . and she fled into the night *(gesture)*

> And the young man? On he ran. Black clouds overhead boiled in rage. To the river! The river!

(Pantomime the following action.)

When he reached that surging stream, the angry sky let loose. Heaven poured down its wrath. Such was the violence of the storm; the riverboat man refused him passage. So he pushed the man aside, and dared to row *himself* across—so great was his shame. *(Frantically rows away.)*

And the woman? On she pressed, blindly stumbling into the mud. Her love, like a beacon in the night, showed her the way. Then the autumn tempest blew a typhoon! Rain, like liquid needles, stabbed her face and arms. Still she pressed on, scarce able to move.

To the river—the river.

Reaching the muddy shore, just as her man pushed off. Swept away from her by the raging waves.

WOMAN. ANATA!!!!!

(She reaches out desperately and freezes. Cross fade as musicians, taiko drummers, and dancers enter.)

(Dramatic musical interlude with all musicians and dancers doing a wild violent dance of repulsion and obsession.)

Scene 5: THE ENDINGS

Tragic Ending

STORYTELLER. And she knelt in the mud until the sound of the riverboat disappeared in the roar of the stream and he was gone. *(She reaches out still blind and crumples to the ground bereft.)*

Romantic Ending

STORYTELLER. But others say that as she knelt there in the mud, she heard the echo of her own heart: "Anata." It was him. The boat had gone but he had stayed. And as he gathered her in his arms, his own bitter tears fell upon her face, and once more she could see. *(Woman feels his face, they embrace, and slowly, happily, they realize she can see.)*

Sacrifice Ending

STORYTELLER. Still others say that in the mud is where the kind innkeeper found her. Sobbing at the edge of the roaring stream. And what if I was to tell you that long ago her father had saved the life of this old man? So that in gratitude, he had watched over her all these years. And how he'd come to admire her faith and he wished that there had been someone in his life to love him like that.

The old man knelt by her side in the mud . . . about to make the supreme sacrifice because it was well known that the human liver is magic medicine.

INNKEEPER. My dear, I owe it to your father to see to your happiness. But I let it slip through my fingers. I am useless . . . Take ye my liver. Make of it a soup. It will restore your sight. *(The innkeeper kills himself, stabbing his belly with the closed fan.)*

Honoring his last request, the woman *(using the fan)* made the soup, drank it *(she drinks it)*, and once more she could see. *(Woman can see but she is desolate.)*

The Best Ending

STORYTELLER. But I believe she sat there in the mud, listening to her man row away. Unable and unwilling to go back! She was stuck in the muck!

I said it was a typhoon! Good lord—the girl was blind! The innkeeper was very, very old; he was back at the inn workin'! Besides, she didn't want his liver, she wanted her lover! And whether or not her man ever came back, I don't know—*(Wait a beat scanning audience.)* Maybe he did—I'm not sure . . . That's the way we all want it to end, don't we? *(Keep asking "don't you?" Until the audience responds.)*

But life don't always work like dat!

This story has been told for a thousand years by a thousand different tellers, in a thousand different ways. How it ends is really up to you, the way you see it.

But if you want my two cents . . .

In the muck, she sat all through that awful night with only the Divine Wind, to keep her company. Rocks and stones pelted her body. Branches tore her face and hair. Still she huddled in the dark, trying to remember the Night of the Firefly Festival and a sweet boy with a love poem and a promise they made . . .

(Dancers enter and dance a final love duet and slowly, painfully separate forever as the woman says the following lines, transitioning from sweet memory to grief to rage all the while singing, weeping, and talking to herself, stuck in the muck in the middle of a typhoon.)

WOMAN. Though I roam away, I'll come back again . . .

He'll come back again. . . . *(The woman tries to console herself.)* He'll come back again cuz I never have proved false.

(The woman, angry now.) I NEVER HAVE PROVED FALSE to the boy I love.

STORYTELLER. And she thought of her father, and the kind innkeeper, and all the people and all the things that had brought her to this moment.

THEN SHE POURED OUT HER SOUL TO THE DIVINE WIND.

WOMAN, *wails like a banshee, like the Divine Wind.*

STORYTELLER, *proclaims like a wise woman, a prophet.* And . . . In the morn, like it always does, the sun rose, slowly at first, then faster and faster. Shining on high, until like a fog lifting . . . *(The woman slowly rises. Defiant.)* Once more, she could see.

(Hold in triumph as lights slowly fade to black.)

CURTAIN

Commentary

"Legend of Morning Glory" is an ancient story from Japan that back before the Kabuki, before the Noh theater, even before the Bunraku puppet plays to the wandering women, the *Shirabyoshi,* who wandered the countryside telling their stories, begging alms for the goddess.

I first heard this story from the great Pete Seeger when I was performing with him and Arlo Guthrie at the Hudson River Rival in New York. Pete told me the story and then began to cry. Now I was very young at the time and in shock to be with folk legends like Pete and Arlo and I didn't know what to do when Pete began to cry. Thirty years later, with a lot more life under my belt, I now know why he cried.

Researching in Japan, I discovered many versions of this story all with different endings. I kept all the endings because a story is like life; it all depends on your perspective. I've done a lot of work with street gangs and at-risk youth, and they identify with the warrior, the princess, and they dream of being rich and long for true love. I want them to be able to perform this story, so I tried to write the characters as those archetypes.

Discussion Questions

1. The format for Brenda Wong Aoki's scripted narrative gives details of voice and notes for the staging of the action. What impact do you think this has on your reading of the story?

2. Consider each scene or "chapter" of the narrative. Describe the one that stood out the most to you. What emotions seemed to be expressed by its characters? How do you think these emotions were most effectively expressed, through words or gestures or both? Share an example by reading or speaking it aloud, with your interpretation of any staging or gestures.

3. Mistakes and misunderstandings are important factors in the plot of this story. Using an "If . . . then" sentence, state one of these mistakes or misunderstandings.

4. We often hear the phrase "looking for true love." What do you think "true love" means? In your opinion, what behaviors and actions are proof of true or real love?

5. The young man in this story never looked for the young woman he claimed to love. What do you think this choice proves about his feelings? Explain your opinion.

6. The young woman in this story continued to wait for a young man who never looked for her. Do you think her choice was faithful, or foolish, or both? Explain your opinion.

7. Legends have their roots in stories of things that really happened. Such stories were once a part of historical narrative shared in the spoken word tradition. Now we can find them in news articles. Find and read two such articles, the first from the *New York Times* (www .nytimes.com/1989/09/08/us/long-beach-journal-eyes-that-saw -horrors-now-see-only-shadows.html), and the second from the *Los Angeles Times* (articles.latimes.com/1989-06-04/news/hl-2445_1_pol -pot-khmer-rouge-blindness).

8. Discuss these articles. Compare the tragic events that led to the princess's blindness, a condition now referred to in medical research as a "conversion disorder." Sometimes conversion disorders can be eased, with support, when the cause is identified and the stress from trauma is relieved. What coping mechanisms do you think the princess had in place? What coping mechanisms do you think she might have developed to relieve the stress of her trauma? What do you think she could have done or said to herself to ease her own troubled mind?

9. Make a connection between a character in this story and a character in some other narrative you have read or viewed, including current news. Describe the similarities and differences between these characters.

10. Consider Aoki's statement in her commentary: "A story is like life; it all depends on your perspective." What does this mean to you?

11. Now, with the previous statement in mind, consider the final scene's alternative endings: the Tragic Ending, the Romantic Ending, the Sacrifice Ending, the Best Ending, and the storyteller's "But if you want my two cents . . ." Which ending do you find most satisfying? Share your perspective on your selection. Or, express another alternative you have in mind.

BRENDA WONG AOKI is a writer, performer, recording artist, and the first nationally recognized Asian American storyteller in the United States. Known for her agility across disciplines and cultures, Brenda has created theatrical works for symphony, jazz ensembles, taiko ensemble, contemporary and traditional world dance, and solo performance. She weaves together Japanese Noh and kyogen theater, dance, and everyday life experience in plays that have been produced in the United States, Japan, China, Singapore, Australia, and Austria. She has been awarded National Endowment Theater Fellowships, Drama-Logue Awards, Indie Awards for Best Spoken Word Recordings, a Critics' Circle Theatre Award, and continued ASCAP Innovation Awards for new libretto. Currently, Brenda is working on a new work, about her mixed-race family's 122-year history in San Francisco, to premiere in 2021, and commissioned by the Hewlett Foundation. Her paternal grandfather was a founder of Japantown in the 1890s, and her maternal grandmother was a leader of the first Chinatown garment union in the 1920s.

Help Yourself: A Folktale from Hawaii

Retold by Nyla Fujii-Babb

The trail between Hilo on the Big Island of Hawaii and the Kau District was long, dry, and hot. Keoha, the old canoe maker, had been walking on the trail for a long time. He was feeling tired and hungry. He had left Hilo yesterday in the cool morning hours, before the sun rose, hoping to finish his business and get home as quickly as possible. He had spent the night in Kau and left much later than he planned. Now he was passing through Puna. He was quite old, and it was already the time of the day when the sun paused at its highest ascent before descending into the afternoon. He had a long way to go before reaching Hilo and home. As he walked, he saw a fisherman carrying his mended nets. "Aloha!" he called.

The fisherman returned the greeting, and as was the custom in those ancient days, asked Keoha if he would like to take a break in his walk to rest and refresh himself.

"Yes, thank you," said Keoha, "I was getting faint from hunger and thirst. A small sip of coconut water would be so good."

"Coconuts," laughed the fisherman, "Yes, I have plenty of those. Come along, it is not very far from here."

Gratefully, Keoha followed the fisherman down a long side trail that led to the beach. He was much hungrier and thirstier, and, by now, felt quite faint. Still the thought of those young coconuts—a cool sip of coconut water, fresh from the shell, and a tiny bit of oil-rich meat—would be so 'ono ka pu'u, refreshing and tasty.

They walked for a long time, the fisherman leading the way and laughing to himself. Finally, they reached the fisherman's village. Nearby was a grove of coconut trees heavily laden with fruit as the fishermen had said. Pointing to the tallest tree in the midst of the grove, the fisherman turned to Keoha and said, "Here are the coconuts. Help yourself!" Still chuckling at the cruel joke he played on the old canoe maker, the fisherman ran up the trail back to his nets.

Keoha was so weary that he sat on the ground and began to weep. Perhaps in his youth he could have climbed the trees and harvested the coconuts, but now he was just too exhausted to go on. He longed for the cool, rain-washed hills of his home in Hilo.

As he sat on the ground trying to gather enough strength to return the way he had come, several young children came up the trail. Having caught some fish, they returned to the village happily chatting about their good day. When they noticed the tired old canoe maker, they quickly made a fire, cleaned, and then roasted their fish. Two of the young boys climbed the coconut trees to harvest the young coconuts. Ramming a sharp stick into the ground, they husked the coconuts over the stick, poked the eyes out of the shells with the end of the stick, and gave one coconut to Keoha to drink. The juice was sweet and cool. With a sharp stone, they split the shell at its seams and scooped out the soft, rich, white meat. Slipping the coconut meat and cooked fish onto a plate made from leaves, the children brought food and more coconut juice to Keoha. They sat with him, making sure that he ate and drank his fill.

With tears of joy replacing his tears of despair, Keoha looked at the children who sat around him, smiling encouragingly at him. "Oh, children," he cried, "you have saved me!" Then he told them of the fisherman's trick.

"We know him, " said the children. "He is selfish and mean and often plays cruel jokes on the people of the village. And he never shares his catch!"

"Someday," said Keoha, "there will come a time to teach that fisherman a lesson." He thanked the children, promising them that if they were ever in Hilo, he would treat them to such a feast!

Several months later, the same fisherman walked into Keoha's village looking for the canoe makers of Hilo. He was led to the workshop of Keoha, the oldest and best of the canoe makers. Not recognizing the old man, the fisherman told Keoha that his fishing canoe had been smashed beyond repair in a storm and he needed a new one right away. "How about that one?" he asked, pointing to a completed canoe drying in the shed.

"Ah, no . . ." paused Keoha, thoughtfully, "that canoe is already spoken for. But I have many canoes in my upland workshop. Come, I will show you."

Taking food and water for both of them, Keoha led the Puna fisherman on a long hike up into the cool mountain forests. The trail was long with many switchbacks, and so steep in places they had to cling to rocks and sturdy bushes along the route. Grumbling, the fisherman said, "How long is this going to take? It is cold and—ugh—wet up here."

In response, Keoha said, "Soon, soon, we are almost there." Finally, after taking a break for food and water, they reached the high mountain forests where the tall, straight koa trees grew. The fine-grained, dark red and golden-colored wood made the finest canoes.

"Here we are," Keoha called out as he pointed to the tallest and most magnificent of the growing trees. "Here is your canoe—help yourself!"

Note: This folktale was originally told by Mary Pukui in her collection, *Tales of the Menehune,* rev. ed. Honolulu: Kamehameha Schools Press, 1985. This version, retold by Nyla Fujii-Babb, was first published in *Skipping Stones: A Multicultural Literary Magazine* 12, no. 4. (2000): 23–24.

Commentary

Hoʻokipa (ho-oh-KEY-pah) translates into English as "hospitality." Like the word *aloha,* this term means much more than can be explained in English. It is a core Native Hawaiian and Polynesian cultural value. Literally the term *kipa* means "to turn from the path." In traditional Polynesian culture, welcoming a visitor into the village and to be a part of your family meant treating the visitor with respect and generosity. In ancient society, there were no fast-food stores or restaurants. People traveled the ancient trails by foot. Villagers were expected to take care of all who traveled along the road with generosity and compassion. Those who were selfish or stingy were considered wicked.

All parts of the coconut tree, *niu* (nee-you), are used in Hawaiian culture. Thatching, drums, rope, brooms, and many other products as well as food come from the coconut tree. Grated or sliced coconut as sold in the stores today comes from the mature fruit or drupe. Mature coconut shells have no liquid in them. When the fruit is young, it contains a potable drink, and the immature flesh inside the shells is soft and edible. Coconut water is the liquid of immature coconut drupes. Coconut milk is made by grating mature coconut and squeezing out the liquid.

Discussion Questions

1. At the end of the story, the Puna fisherman was left with a stand of trees instead of a finished canoe. Predict what happened next: What did he say, what did he do? Do you think he learned his lesson? Did Keoha relent and help him?

2. Keoha had been tricked out of food and drink by the Puna fisherman, but shared water and food with him on the way to the koa grove. Why do you think he did that?

3. What does "hospitality" mean in your family? What kinds of food, drinks, and comforts are offered to visitors?

Of Asian and Native Hawaiian ancestry, "Tutu" ("Grandmother") Nyla's childhood was in the pre-statehood, territorial years of Hawaii. She has been a professional storyteller, artistic director, voice-over talent, librarian, teacher, and actress for over 40 years in Hawaii and on the continental United States. Her many venues include several campuses in the University of Hawaii system, the Aratani Japan America Theatre in Los Angeles, St. Louis, Illinois, and Bay Area festivals, and the National Storytelling Festival as a featured and exchange place teller. She is on the board of Monkey Waterfall, a nonprofit dance/theater company. A retired librarian, Nyla is also adjunct faculty for the Graduate School of Library and Information Science at the University of Hawaii at Manoa.

The Man Who Could Make the Trees Blossom (Hanasaka Jiijii)

Retold by Alton Takiyama-Chung

Mukashi, mukashi aru tokori ni. A long time ago, in ancient Japan, there lived a kind old man and his little dog, Shiro—*Shiro* meaning "white" in Japanese. This kind old man really loved Shiro, and Shiro really loved the kind old man. The kind old man was a farmer, and one day, Shiro began digging in the field and barking, as if to say, "Dig here, Master! Dig here!"

"Oh, Shiro, what have you found there?"

And so the kind old man took his shovel and began to dig where the little dog had been digging, and suddenly, his shovel hit something. *Klunk!* He bent down and cleared away the dirt. It was a large iron pot! He lifted it out. It was heavy. He opened the lid and discovered that it was filled with gold coins. It was a fortune! Someone had buried this pot of gold coins and had forgotten about it. But what should he do with all of this gold?

The kind old man took the pot home and called all of his neighbors in his small farming village to come to his house. There he presented each one with a gold coin. Even after giving away all of that gold, he still had a considerable amount in the pot for himself. Now this was more money than anyone in the village had ever seen, and everyone agreed that this was a wonderful and marvelous thing to do. Everyone, that is, except the mean old man who lived next door.

"Unfair! Unfair! I deserve to have gold, too! I deserve to have gold, too! I know!"

And that mean old man went to the kind old man's house and asked, "May I borrow Shiro just for the afternoon to play?"

Well, the kind old man, being the man that he was, said, "Of course, you may borrow Shiro."

But as soon as he said it, Shiro began to pull at his leash and whine, as if to say, "This is a bad idea, Master! Oh, Master, a very bad idea!"

But the kind old man, had already given his word and, being the man that he was, he said, "Be sure to send Shiro home when you are done playing with him."

"Of course, of course!" said the mean, old man.

He took Shiro's leash and led him into his field. Once out of sight of the kind old man, he lifted up the little dog and said, "All right, Shiro, find me gold!"

Now Shiro was not about to find gold for the mean old man, so he scratched himself, looked at the sky, and yawned. This made the mean old man angry and he threatened Shiro with his shovel. Shiro then got up and sniffed a little here, then moved over there, and then finally, looking at the mean old man, pawed the earth slightly, and then sat down.

The mean old man then tied Shiro to a nearby tree and began digging at the spot where Shiro had pawed the earth. "Rut-roh!"

As soon as he began digging, Shiro began to pull at his leash and whine. Then the mean old man's shovel hit something. *Klunk!* He knelt down and cleared away the dirt.

But what he found was not an iron pot. What he found were rags, bones, and bits of pottery. And then oozing, oily, thick black liquid began to fill the hole. It smelled bad and stained everything it touched.

The mean old man got angry. He got so angry that he hit Shiro over the head with his shovel and killed him. "Oh, no! Oh, no! Now what do I do? Ahh! I know!"

And the mean old man picked up the body of Shiro and went to the kind old man's house. "Sorry! Sorry! Terrible accident! Terrible accident!" he said. He left the body of the dog on the kind old man's doorstep and scuttled away.

Now the kind old man was devastated. Here was the body of his best friend. He took Shiro into his house and cleaned him up. He sat up with him all night long, talking to him, praying for him, crying over him, and said good-bye to his old friend.

At last, in the morning, he dug a grave in the yard that he and Shiro loved so well. He wrapped his friend in a nice blanket and buried him in the garden. The last thing the kind old man did was to plant a small pine tree over the grave of his friend. He took care of that sapling and watered it every day. And don't you know that something magical happened.

That pine tree, which was just a sapling, grew into an enormous tree in a matter of months. It grew so big that a grown man could not put his arms around its trunk. Now it was the middle of December, and the icy, cold wind was blowing through the branches of that tree. The kind old man looked up at that tree and he could almost hear the voice of his old friend say, "Oh, Master! Master! Cut me down, Master! Make something useful of me, Master! Oh, Master!"

"You know," said the kind old man, "it is almost New Year's. I will cut this pine tree down, make a mochi mortar, and make mochi, in honor of Shiro! He always liked mochi!"

In Japan, they celebrate the New Year by making mochi. They get a large block of wood, hollow out a bowl-size depression in it, and fill it with hot, sticky rice. Such a mochi mortar is called an usu. They then get a large wooden mallet called a kine and bring it down on the rice. They keep mashing it, turning it, and adding water till they have something that has the consistency of taffy. This they form into little balls that they flatten and eat. It is a traditional dish to welcome in the New Year.

And that is what the kind old man did. He chopped down the huge pine tree and made a mochi mortar out of the trunk and a wooden mallet from one of the larger limbs. When it was finished, he filled it with hot, sticky rice and brought the kine down on the hot, sticky rice. There was a *poof*, and rice scattered across the floor. Not hot, sticky rice, but fine, dry rice. He brought the mallet down again and *poof*, more dry rice scattered to the floor. Soon there was an endless cascade of dry rice erupting from the usu, the mochi mortar, onto the floor. The kind old man scooped the rice into a bag and filled it. He grabbed another and another, and soon he had enough rice to last him an entire year. Now, not only did he have gold, but he also had food to last him a long time. He thought that this was absolutely wonderful and marvelous, and it was, except that the mean old man next door was looking through a hole in the fence.

"Unfair! Unfair! I deserve to have rice, too! I deserve to have rice, too! Ahh! I know!"

And the mean old man went to the kind old man, "May I borrow your usu and kine, for I, too, would like to make mochi in honor of Shiro." And the kind old man, being the man that he was, loaned the mochi mortar and mallet to his neighbor.

The mean old man took the mochi mortar to his house and filled it with hot, sticky rice. But when he brought the mochi mallet down on the hot, sticky rice, fine dry rice did not come out of the mortar. Instead, what flew out were bits of rags, bone, and bits of pottery, and then an oozing, oily, thick black liquid flowed out of the mochi mortar. It stained everything it touched, and it smelled horribly.

The mean old man got angry. He got so angry that he got his axe and he chopped up that mochi mortar into pieces, but he wasn't through yet! He took all of those pieces and threw them into the fireplace. And he burned them in the fireplace—he burned them all to ashes.

When the kind old man came to reclaim his mochi mortar, the mean old man pointed to his fireplace and said, "There it is! Bah!" and he scuttled away.

Now the kind old man was heartbroken. Here was the last remembrance of his friend, so he scooped up some of the ash into a little bucket and took it home. He was going to spread the ash around the garden that he and his little friend had loved so well.

But don't you know that something magical happened! As soon as he spread a handful of ash about the garden, *poof!* The entire garden burst into bloom. Here it was, the middle of winter when everything is cold, gray, and dark. And suddenly, everything in the garden was green, and all of the flowers blossomed. People came from miles around to view this miracle.

Now, the lord of the area, the person who ruled over this part of Japan, had a cherry tree in his garden, which he had planted as a boy. The last winter had been an especially hard one, and the tree had died. He heard about the kind old man and asked him to come to his house to see what he could do for his beloved tree. The kind old man climbed into the branches and he cast a handful of the magic ash into branches of the cherry tree. As soon as he did, *poof,* the tree burst into bloom.

The tree was covered with delicate pink and white flowers, and the lord was very pleased. He gave the kind old man gifts of rare silk, pieces of art, and more gold. He also gave the kind old man a title. From now on, he would be known as Sir, the Man Who Could Make the Trees Blossom. This was a great honor, for now the kind old man was a member of the aristocracy. People came from miles around to visit him, present him with gifts, and ask his advice. Everyone in the little village thought that this was a wonderful and marvelous thing. Everyone, that is, except the mean old man who lived next door.

"Unfair! Unfair! I deserve to have a title, too! I deserve to have a title, too! Ahhh! I know!" And with that, the mean old man scooped up the rest of that ash from his fireplace into a bucket and went out to the main road.

Well, it just so happened that the lord was touring the area with his soldiers. The mean old man ran out in front of them and began throwing handfuls of ash into the bare trees on either side of the road, saying, "I can make the trees blossom, too! I can make the trees blossom, too!"

But, wouldn't you know, something magical happened. Just then, a breeze sprung up and blew all of that ash into the faces of the lord and his soldiers. The lord got angry. He got so angry.

"Guards! Arrest that man!"

And the mean old man was seized.

"What is the meaning of this?"

He was so scared. He was so scared that he told the lord everything, about how he had killed Shiro, how he had chopped up the mochi mortar, and how he had burned it to ashes.

The lord was very angry and sent the mean old man away to jail for a very long time. But when he returned, he was a changed man. He went back to the kind old man, apologized, and made amends. He made amends, and every year, at New Year's, these two old men would get together and make mochi, in honor of Shiro.

Commentary

My grandmother came to Hawaii from Japan as a picture bride, and I grew up with my mother telling me this old folktale. Now, as an adult, I have come back to it with new eyes. In researching this story, I discovered that there are many versions, each emphasizing various aspects of Japanese culture. In some versions, the kind old man shares his gold with the entire village, illustrating altruism and emphasizing the value of community. In some versions, both old men have wives, but no children. In one version, the mortar produces rice instead of gold and the old man and his wife never go hungry again. This illustrates the importance of rice to Japanese culture. Rice is a staple of every meal. The word *gohan* means "cooked rice," as well as "meal." From the 16th to the middle of the 19th century, rice was used as currency in Japan.

It is a New Year's tradition for Japanese families to eat or make mochi or rice cakes. *Mochitsuki,* pounding of the rice cakes, is essential to the *Oshogatsu,* or Japanese New Year's celebration. It takes the cooperation of many people to grow the rice and to make mochi. Traditionally, mochi is set out as an offering to the gods and ancestors, and making mochi is a way of acknowledging the life-giving sustenance of rice. The whole concept of taking rice, this precious commodity, making it into a special treat, and sharing it with others, sets the mood for prosperity and community strength for the coming year.

Pounding mochi is a spiritual metaphor: melding thousands of grains of rice, each representing a separate, individual soul, into a single whole, where it is impossible to determine where one person begins and another ends. Through this communal effort, community is formed, bonds between individuals are created, and ties are made, linking the present to the past.

In some versions of this traditional Japanese folktale, the old man sits with the body of Shiro all night long, showing respect for the dead. Some listeners may find the cruelty done to Shiro distasteful, but the story itself revolved around the spirit of Shiro transcending that experience and coming back time and time again to bring prosperity to his old master and disappointment to his murderer. Shiro talks to the kind old man in some versions, and even after death, instructs the old man to make something useful from his tree, indicating a belief in life after death.

The mean old man is sent away to prison for his crimes in some versions and comes back a better man. In one version, the mean old man is threatened with prison and makes amends with the kind old man. They become friends, and both come together in remembrance each year on the anniversary of Shiro's death. *Shiro* means "white," the color often associated with death and magical happenings.

The kind old man never retaliates against his mean neighbor, demonstrating forbearance and forgiveness. The renaming of the old man by the lord or magistrate is significant in that the kind old man not only gains wealth, but also honor and prestige. He is reborn. He is no longer a commoner and is raised in social rank, which affords privilege and wealth. This is of tremendous significance, because very little upward mobility occurred between social classes in ancient Japan.

The cherry blossoms are significant in that they are very beautiful, but last for only a short time, illustrating the beauty, mystery, and ephemeral quality of life. Cherry blossoms bloom in spring and herald a time of awakening and promise after a cold, gray winter of introspection. Dark, dormant trees erupt with color and life, but in a few short days, showers of delicate pink and white petals all too soon give way to new leaves. A haiku poem attributed to Admiral Onishi speaks to the impermanence of life:

In blossom today, then scattered.
Life is so like a delicate flower.
How can one expect the fragrance to last forever?

Japanese people are very conscious of seasonal changes, and the *hanami* (cherry blossom viewing) is one of the most popular customs. When cherry blossoms are in bloom, people spread out picnic mats and enjoy themselves while celebrating the arrival of spring. The origin of hanami dates back to Heian period (794–1191), when the aristocrats at court held parties to enjoy the beauty of *sakura* (cherry blossoms). Over the course of centuries, the custom spread to the warrior class (samurai), but it wasn't until the Edo period (1603–1867) that hanami became popular among the common people.

In Japan and in some areas of the United States, the blooming of cherry trees is celebrated with a festival, the *Sakura Matsuri,* or Cherry Blossom Festival. These festivals are often held to promote Japanese culture and traditions. The message of the cherry blossom is that beauty and life are fleeting and that it is important to live in the moment and to live well, holding eternal spring in your heart.

Resources

McAlpine, Helen, and William McAlpine. *Japanese Tales and Legends.* Oxford, England: Oxford University Press, 1958.
Ozaki, Yei Theodora. *The Japanese Fairy Book.* Tokyo: Tuttle Publishing, 1970.
Sakade, Florence. *Little One-Inch and Other Japanese Children's Favorite Stories.* Tokyo: Charles E. Tuttle Company, 1958.

Discussion Questions

1. What traditions or special foods do you have in your home at certain times of the year? Do you know where these traditions came from?

2. Folktales often teach people how they should behave. Given this story, what can you conclude about how Japanese people should or should not behave toward each other?

3. Given this story, what can you conclude about that which would be most honored and respected in Japanese culture?

Japanese and Korean storyteller ALTON TAKIYAMA-CHUNG grew up with the stories, superstitions, and magic of the Hawaiian Islands. This gives him a unique perspective when telling cultural tales and personal stories of growing up in Hawaii, stories of the Japanese American experience of WWII, Asian folktales, and Hawaiian legends. He was awarded the National Storytelling Network's first J.J. Reneaux Emerging Artist Award. Performances include the Timpanogos Storytelling Festival, the Cayman Islands Gimme Story Storytelling Festival, Singapore's Asian Congress of Storytellers, and the International Storytelling Festival of Thailand. He has also been the Teller-in-Residence at the International Storytelling Center and a Featured Teller at the National Storytelling Festival. His DVD, *Life is the Treasure: Okinawan Memories Of WWII,* and CD, *Tales from the Lanai,* have both won Storytelling World Honors. He is also the former chairman of the board of directors of National Storytelling Network.

Boundless Strength: A Japanese Legend

Retold by Motoko

Daikichi woke up shivering, although the air was not cold in the late-spring evening. He kept his eyes closed, in order to avoid looking at himself in his deplorable condition, but he knew exactly where he was. Slumped on the ground in a drunken stupor against a wooden wall in a dark, deserted alley. Unshaven, dirty, and dazed. Homeless. Worthless. Penniless.

Well, almost penniless. Daikichi felt in his kimono sleeve for the silver coin the sleazy pawnshop owner had handed to him, in exchange for his last sword. Did he detect pity in the obsequious man's eyes? Never in his life had Daikichi imagined he would pawn his swords, the symbol of his honor and pride as a young samurai!

With his eyes still closed, Daikichi tried to remember himself only a year ago: a stout, powerful warrior loyally serving Lord Tomura in his magnificent castle. Daikichi's particular strength was in sumo wrestling. He loved practicing close combat and was much respected for his skills. Every autumn he was the star wrestler at the local rice harvest festival. Sumo tournaments were held as a ceremony of gratitude for the bountiful crop and of hope for prosperity in the coming year. In his mind, Daikichi could still hear the sigh of admiration from the spectators, as he solemnly stomped on the ground and scattered purifying salt over the arena in the pre-bout ritual.

"Hakke-yoi! Nokotta nokotta!" the referee would intone, holding up a ceremonial fan.

The crowd roared as Daikichi lifted his opponent's massive body off the ground and ousted him from the ring.

None of that, however, mattered any longer.

If only Lord Tomura had not passed away so suddenly! What seemed like a common cold progressed into an infection that claimed his master's life. If only there had been a male heir! Without a son to carry on the clan name, the grieving family fell into the hands of its political enemies. The castle was taken over by another clan. The family was dispersed. Those who had been serving with loyal hearts were dismissed and scattered. End of story.

Oh, the unfairness of it all! Now that the enemies of his late master were in power, there was no position for Daikichi. He was a *ronin,* a warrior with no master, no purpose in life. Bitterness and fury drove him to drink. At first it seemed that drinking had gained him some new friends, or so he thought. It turned out they were no friends at all, but hawkeyed gamblers. His meager savings were gone before long. So were his swords . . . and his strength.

Now he had to find a place to spend the night before he got robbed on the street. There were people even more desperate than he was.

His eyes flew open. Startled by sudden, explosive barks, he leapt to his feet. A young woman rushed into the alley, closely chased by three big, wild mongrels. They cornered their prey against a wall, ready to pounce. Their hungry eyes and sharp teeth glittered in the dark. The woman's screams pierced the night as she cowered, covering her face with her kimono sleeves.

Daikichi frantically looked around. He saw a pile of discarded lumber and grabbed a long, thick stick. He jumped in between the woman and the dogs, swinging with a battle-worthy strength. In that moment, he was a samurai again.

"Get! Get!" He yelled. The wood made contact with satisfying whacks. The furry beasts ran away, yelping in pain.

Daikichi dropped the stick and turned. The woman lay on the ground, still trembling. Her long black hair had come loose, spread in disarray over her slender shoulders.

"Are you all right?" Daikichi knelt down beside her. She looked up.

"Yes. Thank you, sir, for saving my life." Her voice was clear and resonant. Her smile made her pale face glow faintly in the moonlight.

Her name was Kayo. She was a young widow, who owned a little teashop nearby. When she found out that Daikichi was homeless, she invited him to stay at her house. Daikichi hesitated. He knew it might be considered inappropriate. What would her neighbors say? He certainly did not want to impose and did not intend to be disrespectful in any way. Yet, anything was better than sleeping in the alley. He had already hit rock bottom. He surely was not in a position to worry about reputation, his own or hers.

In the end, Daikichi accepted, mostly because of the way Kayo seemed to completely accept and trust him. His shameful condition did not seem to bother her at all. Neither did the thought of her neighbors' meddlesome talk. She was a woman with a mind of her own, a rare blend of innocence, determination, and genuine kindness.

Her teashop bought and sold green tea leaves from various parts of Japan. Daikichi loved being in the clean, cozy store filled with sweet fragrance. He forswore drinking and gambling, and began helping Kayo in the shop. Every day, he concentrated on memorizing the names of different kinds of tea, and tried not to think about his past, or his swords in the pawnshop. At night, in Kayo's embrace, he found comfort and affection he did not even believe he deserved.

Many moons passed. The harvest was plentiful. Their tea business, however, was struggling. Daikichi kept himself busy by taking over more and more responsibilities in the shop, learning the way of a merchant. Being a proud samurai was a distant memory pushed into a far corner of his heart.

One crisp, autumn morning, Daikichi and Kayo were sitting down to breakfast. A simple, blessed meal of steamed rice and bean curd soup. Kayo abruptly got up and left the room. Daikichi followed and was alarmed to find her doubled over on the *tatami* (straw mats), moaning with nausea.

"Kayo! Are you alright? What is the matter?" He knelt down to support her.

Kayo leaned into his arms and looked up. On her face he again saw the enchanting smile.

"Daikichi-san, we are going to have a baby," Kayo whispered.

"W-w-what?!"

In the moment it took him to understand her meaning, it felt as if the floor beneath him was crumbling. Nearly crushed under the burden of an uncertain future, he stammered, "Are . . . are you sure? I mean, I don't think it will work . . ."

"But Daikichi-san, I thought you would be happy."

"Happy?! How could I be happy? Look at me. I'm in no condition to take care of you and the baby. What do you want from me?"

"Daikichi-san! Wait!"

He was not proud of the disgraceful way he turned on his heel. He just needed time to think, in solitude, he kept telling himself. Yet, there was no place for him to go. He aimlessly roamed around the town till dusk. What was he running from? Where was he heading to? Nothing seemed certain anymore.

A small, makeshift tavern with wooden benches caught his eye. His empty stomach growled at the delicious smell of grilled bean curd. Like a moth to a flame, he staggered over and sat at the end of a bench. A cup of hot sake might soothe his ragged nerves, he hoped.

"Hey! Did I tell you about Lord Hiraga's amazing sumo tournament?"

A voice rose from a group of men drinking together nearby. Daikichi's ears perked up.

"Yeah, you've told us already, but nobody believes you," another man slurred.

"What do you mean, you don't believe me? I just came back from Lord Hiraga's city. It took me three days!" the first man argued.

"The part we don't believe is," a third man chimed in, "what you said about the reward money. One hundred gold coins? Who's got that much money to give away?"

"Lord Hiraga does, you ignorant fools! He is the richest *daimyo* north of the Mogami River. I swear to you, the reward for the champion will be one hundred gold coins!"

"In that case, I'm going," a fourth man slammed his empty cup on the bench, "I will be a rich man!"

"Yeah, right. They'll whop your skinny butt in no time!" The men broke into a raucous laughter.

Daikichi left the tavern and hurried home. As if driven by an invisible force, he quickly packed and left again without any explanation.

Kayo's bewildered face stayed with him, but he tried to focus on the task at hand. A three-day journey brought him to the city ruled by the powerful Lord Hiraga. Young men from all over the region milled about, each one sporting hard muscles and a hot temper. Colorful banners with Hiraga's family crest swayed in the cloudless sky. A round arena was set up in front of Lord Hiraga's mansion.

Many men waited in a long line for their turn to show their worth. The line stretched from the arena onto the street and across a bridge. Daikichi joined the line on the far end of the bridge and inched his way forward.

As he stood, however, he could not help but notice all the other men were in much better shape than he was. He was once a famous wrestler, but that seemed like a lifetime ago. Was he about to make a complete fool of himself? He felt utterly out of shape, out of place.

But he needed the gold . . .

Daikichi reached the middle of the bridge. He peered into the sparkling stream below. Suddenly, someone called his name.

"Daikichi-san?"

He spun around and saw a small, silver-haired woman in an indigo blue kimono. He had never seen her before. How did she know his name? She was holding a baby wrapped in white silk. She looked up at his face and spoke in an earnest tone, "Would you please hold this baby for me? I will be right back. Please promise that you won't drop him or put him down."

Daikichi had no idea who the old lady was, or where she was going, or why she had picked him out of the long line of men, but he heard something serious and urgent in her voice. He simply agreed, "Okay, I promise," and willingly took the baby in his arms. The old woman smiled, bowed deeply, and quickly went away.

Daikichi looked at the baby. It was a tiny newborn, sleeping quietly. He thought about Kayo and his child in her womb. How terrifyingly mysterious human life was! How hopelessly ill-equipped he would be as a father . . .

A curious, unexpected sensation overcame him. It felt as if the baby in his arms suddenly grew bigger. He looked down, but the baby had not changed in size. Another sensation. The baby still in a peaceful slumber.

Chills spread down his spine as Daikichi realized what was happening. Without changing its size, the baby was growing heavier. It started out weighing no more than 7 pounds, but now it was 15, 20 pounds. Then it became 30 pounds, 50 pounds. . . .

"I've been tricked!" Daikichi broke into a cold sweat. This baby was not human. The old woman was probably a demon, out to do evil and mischief! He was ready to throw the baby into the river. At the last moment, however, he remembered his promise.

"I used to be a samurai," he muttered to himself.

"No, I am still a samurai," he said louder. "A samurai never breaks his promise."

The baby was rapidly gaining weight. Soon it was more than a hundred pounds, then two hundred. Daikichi was no longer able to stand. He knelt down on the ground and felt as if his knees, shoulders, and arms were breaking. Sweat poured down from his face. He clenched his teeth tightly. Three hundred pounds, four hundred pounds. . . . Still, he refused to let go.

The old woman still did not come back. Meanwhile, the line ahead of him was moving along. Daikichi knew his turn to fight was coming closer. Men lined up behind him impatiently urged him to move on, but he could not. Finally, they started moving past him, laughing at him for bringing a baby to the tournament.

Daikichi tried with all his might not to be overwhelmed by the baby's weight, but the pressure was far too much to bear. He thought he would faint right on the spot.

All at once, out of nowhere, the old woman reappeared. She effortlessly lifted the child from Daikichi's arms and stood regally in front of him. Daikichi looked up, exhausted and stupefied.

"Thank you, Daikichi-san, for your kind help!" the woman beamed, "I am the *ujigami*, the guardian goddess of this city.

"Today I had to help a poor farmer's wife give birth. The labor was excruciating. The baby took forever to come. That is why I needed your assistance.

"If you had let go of this infant, both the farmer's wife and their child would have died. However, because you kept your promise, they both survived. As a token of my appreciation I give you, your children, and your children's children the gift of boundless strength." She reached over and touched Daikichi's sweat-streaked cheek.

"Now it's time for you to go and wrestle in the tournament," the old woman whispered with a twinkle in her eye. Then she and the baby vanished into thin air.

Daikichi rose, as if awakened from a dream. He registered himself and disrobed. Clad only in a white loincloth, he entered the wrestling arena. The powerful Lord Hiraga and his retinue watched, seated on a high platform draped with a bright red carpet. His first opponent, a burly, bull-like man sneered from across the ring.

"Hey, babysitter! Where's your baby?" Everyone laughed.

Daikichi took a deep breath and stomped lightly on the ground to warm up. Instantly he realized what he had gone through had been no dream. The earth shook under his feet. His opponent lost his balance and landed on his buttocks! Everyone, including Daikichi, was speechless.

"Who . . . who is this man?!" Lord Hiraga leaned in to watch.

"*Hakke yoi!*" the referee signaled the beginning of the match.

A mysterious energy coursed through Daikichi's veins. His physical power was so immense that the smallest effort was enough to overcome his challengers. Not wishing to cause any injury, Daikichi quickly learned to do the gentlest moves. All day long, the other wrestlers charged. All day long, Daikichi lifted them out of the ring as if he was wrestling with little children.

Lord Hiraga declared Daikichi the champion, and bestowed upon him one hundred gold coins. The crowd cheered wildly. They praised Daikichi and wanted to celebrate with him, but Daikichi did not stay. He hurried home, back to where his heart belonged.

"I knew you would be back," Kayo gave him that familiar smile.

"I am ready," Daikichi smiled back, finally at peace with himself, knowing he was strong enough to become a father.

The legend tells us they lived happily ever after. It is also said, even to this day, that descendants of Daikichi and Kayo always possess boundless strength.

Commentary

The story is based on a legend from a region in Akita Prefecture formerly known as Dewa no kuni, in northwestern part of Japan's Honshu Island. Another version of the same legend, called "The Story of Umetsu Chube," is available in English in Lafcadio Hearn's 1901 book titled *A Japanese Miscellany* (Kessinger Publishing, 2007).

Men and women of medieval Japan struggled to survive wars, poverty, natural disasters, military dictatorships, and a sexist, patriarchal culture. Folktales and legends often tell us about the sources of the people's strength, resilience, and enjoyment of life: family, community, religions and beliefs, spiritual practices, arts, and sports. This tale encourages us to explore what makes humans strong beyond their physical abilities. It also reminds us that, before the advancement in modern medicine, childbirth was a perilous, and often fatal, ordeal for women. Maternal deaths were so common in medieval and premodern Japan that pregnancy and childbirth were often referred to as *onna no ikusa,* "a woman's battle."

The following information may help further readers' understanding of the tale.

The samurai (also called *bushi)* were the warrior class that rose to prominence during the 12th century. Various regional clans fought against one another to gain the political ruling power based on a feudal economy. The head of the prevailing clan became the *shogun,* who established the government called the *shogunate,* formally endorsed by the imperial court.

The *daimyo* were feudal lords subordinate to the shogun. Usually of the samurai class, the daimyo ruled their hereditary landholdings and hired armies of samurai to guard and fight for them. This system of feudal military dictatorship lasted until the end of the Tokugawa shogunate in 1868, when the political sovereignty was restored to the emperor.

Sumo is an ancient Japanese tradition, and is considered Japan's national sport. It originated more than 1,500 years ago as part of the Shinto ritual for rice harvest. In sumo, two wrestlers, clad only in loincloths, face off in the middle of a round arena measuring 4.55 meters (about 15 feet) in diameter. Sumo wrestlers range in weight, anywhere from 200 to 500 pounds.

To encourage the wrestlers during the match, the referee shouts, *"Hakke yoi nokotta nokotta!"* (meaning "Try your hardest! It's not over yet!"). The first wrestler to force his opponent to fall within the ring or step out of the ring wins. Each bout usually lasts less than two minutes.

Shinto is the native religion of Japan. It is an animistic polytheism that focuses on performing rituals to connect humans with *kami,* numerous spirits who reside in nature. Sumo, from its inception, has been closely related to Shinto and has preserved many ancient traditions, such as the use of salt purification in the pre-bout protocol. The Shinto philosophy and practices grew to incorporate various elements, such as ancestor worship, Taoism, Buddhism, and reverence for the imperial family.

An *ujigami* is a guardian deity of a particular village or community. Members of a community belonged to the same Shinto shrine, participated in the same rituals, and shared responsibilities for one another. They prayed to their ujigami for good harvests, health, success, and protection from evil spirits.

Discussion Questions

1. Why do people play sports? What have you learned from playing a sport?
2. How do you define human strength? What makes a human strong beyond his or her physical capabilities?
3. Discuss ways people recover from failure, defeat, or loss of identity or status.
4. In our cultures, how do people prepare themselves for parenthood?

The recipient of the National Storytelling Network's 2017 Circle of Excellence Award, MOTOKO has enchanted audiences of every age since 1993. Her repertoire includes Asian folktales, rakugo and Zen tales, ghost stories, mime vignettes, as well as oral memoirs from her childhood in Osaka, Japan, and her life as an immigrant in the United States. Her latest work includes "RADIANT: Stories from Fukushima," an original one-woman multimedia performance on Japan's 2011 nuclear power plant meltdown. As a teaching artist, Motoko has been awarded numerous grants for her arts in education programs on creative writing, Japanese culture, ancient China, and origami geometry. Her story recordings have won a Parents' Choice Silver Honor Award, a Storytelling World Award, and a National Parenting Publications Award. She is the author of *A Year in Japan: Folktales, Songs and Art for the Classroom*. For more on Motoko, visit www.folktales.net.

3

Voices Carried West from Europe to the Span of Two American Continents

The Time Jack Went to Seek His Fortune

Retold by Donald Davis

One time, Jack was living all alone with his mother. They lived in a little house in the mountains, and life was awful hard for them. Jack's big brothers, Tom and Will, had already gone off from home to look for their fortunes. Jack wasn't much help at all to his mama there at home.

One day Jack came to his mother and told her, "Mama," he said, "we're having such a time of trouble that I think it's about time for me to get on out of here and seek my fortune. Tom and Will must have found theirs by now because they never have come back home. I think it is about time for me to go and look for mine."

"That's a good idea, Jack," his mother said. "You have to do it sometime, so it might as well be now."

After breakfast the next morning Jack started out walking down the road.

There was just one problem: all of a sudden Jack realized that he didn't know what a fortune was. All he knew was that his brothers had left home to seek theirs and if they had done it then he could do it too. So, he was looking, but he didn't know what he was looking for.

Jack thought, Well, I don't know what my fortune is, but I guess I'll know it when I see it. He looked all through the countryside and then all through the town. He never did see anything that he thought looked like his fortune.

After a couple of days, Jack thought, I'm going to starve to death if I don't find my fortune pretty soon. I guess I'm going to have to stop looking for a while and get a job so I can buy me something to eat.

Jack began looking for work and before long he found a farmer who was in need of a helper on the farm.

"You're in luck, Jack," the farmer said. "You can work for me, and besides that you can stay right here and sleep and eat at our house with us."

Jack was surely pleased by this. At least now he wouldn't starve to death.

The farmer went on talking, "Since you're going to eat and sleep at our house, you won't need any money as the days go along, Jack. So, I'll just save up what you earn and when you're ready to go on your way, I'll pay you for the time you've worked here all at once. That ought to help you out."

Jack didn't care about money one way or the other. All he wanted was to have some food and a sleeping place so he could look for his fortune.

Before Jack knew how much time had passed, he had worked and slept and eaten at the farmer's house for a full year, and he was not even interested in leaving. Time went on and on like that, and one day Jack woke up and realized that he had been working for the farmer for seven years!

He sat up in bed and said right out loud to himself. "I've got to get on out of here! I left home to seek my fortune and this job is holding me up. I will never find my fortune if I have to keep working all the time. I am seven years behind already and I need to get moving."

Jack told the farmer and his wife that he would be leaving the next day so he could get on his way looking for his fortune.

Jack went down to breakfast the next morning, and right there in the middle of the kitchen floor he saw a two-bushel basket filled to the brim with money. It was quarters and dimes and nickels and a whole lot of pennies. Jack figured that the basket of money must weigh over five hundred pounds. He had never seen so much money in all his life. At least he wouldn't starve to death while he was looking for his fortune.

After breakfast Jack started trying to move that basket of money out to the road so he could get on his way. It took all day. He pulled and pushed and shoved and strained until by lunchtime he had it out the door and down the steps into the yard. After a little rest, it took Jack the entire afternoon to get the basket of money on out to the side of the road.

Just about dark Jack went back up to the farmer's house. "I'm not making much progress," he told the farmer. "All of that money you gave me is holding me up. Unless I can find some way to get rid of it, why, I will never be able to get on with looking for my fortune."

The next morning Jack said good-bye for the second time. He went out to the side of the road and sat down beside the money so he could think for a while.

In about an hour he heard someone coming down the road and looked up to see a man approaching in a two-wheeled buggy being pulled by a pretty fine-looking horse. Jack had an idea: "If I had a horse and buggy like that, I really would be able to get on to seeking my fortune."

Jack waved to the man in the buggy and got him to stop. "Hello," he said, "Would you be willing to swap that horse and buggy for this basket of money I've got here? It's keeping me from looking for my fortune."

The traveler looked at the basket of money and realized that there was enough there to buy a really good team of horses and a brand-new four-wheeled buggy. He looked at Jack and said, "Well, I guess I'd be willing to trade with you. Would it be an even swap?"

"Only if you take every last cent of this money," Jack said. "I've just got to get rid of it."

After a few days Jack realized that he had made a mistake. Not only was he making no progress at all in figuring out what his fortune might look like, but he was having to find food for his new horse as well as for himself. It sure was a heap of trouble.

"I've got to get rid of this horse and buggy," he thought out loud. "They are no help at all and are really holding me up from looking for my fortune."

The next day Jack was going down the road when he met a woman who was leading a cow to town to sell her.

"Now, that is just what I need," Jack figured. "If I had that cow, I would have plenty of milk to drink, and the cow would just eat grass along the side of the road and feed herself."

"Hello," Jack said to the woman. "How would you like to trade me that cow for this horse and buggy?"

The woman could hardly believe it. She knew that the horse and buggy had to be worth a half-dozen cows.

"You mean," she went on, "that I could get the horse and buggy for just this one cow?"

"That's right," answered Jack, "but you have to take both of them or it is no deal. You see, they are slowing me down from seeking my fortune, and I need to get them on out of the way." And so, Jack traded the horse and buggy for one milk cow.

Two days later Jack realized that he had made a big mistake. The old cow was dry and he never got a single drop of milk from her. Besides that, she didn't like eating grass along beside the road. No, the cow was always running off and getting right into people's cornfields.

"I have got to get rid of this old cow," Jack said to himself. "I will never find my fortune as long as I keep having to chase after her."

It was in the afternoon of the very next day that Jack caught up with a young girl who was carrying a hen under her arm. She had helped a neighbor woman spring-clean her house and the hen was what she had been paid for several days of work.

"Now, that is just what I need," Jack said out loud when he saw the hen. "I could get eggs to eat every day and it surely wouldn't take much to feed one old hen."

It didn't take much convincing for the girl to agree to trade the hen for the cow. A cow was a lot better pay for housecleaning than one old hen could ever be. Jack started down the road, still looking for his fortune, with the hen under his arm.

Before that one day was over, Jack knew that he was in a fix. He didn't even know that hen hadn't laid an egg in over a year, but he did know that he had to carry her every step that he took. He knew that he had to get rid of her.

Maybe, Jack thought, Maybe I can trade this old hen for something to eat. Then I won't starve to death while I am seeking my fortune.

The first place where Jack saw any activity was a blacksmith shop. He walked inside with his hen under his arm, determined to trade her for something to keep him from starving.

The blacksmith was hammering on a horseshoe. When he stopped and looked up, Jack started in on his bargaining. "Sir," he said to the blacksmith," I am out seeking my fortune, but things keep getting in my way. Now, take this hen here. I don't really need her, and I wonder if I could trade her to you for something to eat?"

The man looked up and down at Jack and finally he said, "Well, son, I could trade you some victuals for that hen, but that wouldn't be fair. Why, you'd eat up that food in no time and then you'd be out of food and I'd still have your hen.

"What you need is something that would feed you for a good long time. I'll trade you something that you can use to make enough money each day so that you can buy food from now on. What do you think of that?"

Jack was awfully pleased. He handed that hen right over to the blacksmith and waited to see what he was going to get in return for it.

The blacksmith took the old hen out the back door of his shop and put her under a tin tub where he could come back and wring her neck and cook her once Jack was gone and out of the way. Then he went out to the edge of his garden and scrounged up two good-size yellow flint rocks. He washed them in the horse trough and oiled them up until they were nice and shiny.

Jack was waiting when the blacksmith came back in the shop door and flopped the two rocks down on the workbench in front of him. "Here you are, Jack!" he announced.

Then he went on, "These here are nail-straightening rocks. You put a bent nail on top of one of these rocks and then you hit it with the other one until the bent nail turns out straight. There are people in every house in the countryside who have bent nails that they would like to have straightened. If you go from house to house, you can get paid good money for straightening people's crooked nails for them. Now, go to it, Jack, and good luck with your fortune."

Jack picked up the nail-straightening rocks and started out the door. He felt pretty good about his last trade because, even though he had never seen nail-straightening rocks before, he knew that he wouldn't have to feed them anything. He started down the road on the lookout for his first nail-straightening customers.

As Jack walked down the road, the first house he came to had a big covered well right out in the front yard. It was a very hot day, and, as Jack headed up toward the house, he stopped by the well to draw him a good drink of water.

He put his nail-straightening rocks down on the side of the well, dropped the bucket down into the well, and started to pull the bucket of water up working hand over hand. Just as the bucket got to the top, one of Jack's elbows by accident hit the nail-straightening rocks and knocked both of them right down into the well. Jack heard them splash as they hit the water and then sank on down to the bottom.

He took a good long drink of water. Then Jack stood up straight and smiled from ear to ear.

"I must be the luckiest fellow in the world!" Jack proclaimed right out loud. "I started out looking for my fortune, and for seven years I was held up by having a job. Once I got out of that, I was held up by having so much money that I couldn't tote it. As soon as I got rid of the money, I had to feed a horse and take care of it, then I had to manage a cow that was always running off, then I had to carry a hen that didn't even lay eggs, and then two big rocks that I had to carry everywhere . . .

"But now . . . now I can really go looking for my fortune because I don't have one single thing that is standing in my way and holding me up. Yes, I am the luckiest fellow in the world!"

And so, Jack started off down the road again, still not knowing what his fortune was, but awfully happy to be looking for it.

Commentary

The focus of this Jack tale centers around the meaning of the word *fortune.*

We often hear that, historically, people have emigrated from one part of the world to another to "seek their fortune." But, what does that mean, and how is the meaning different from one group of people to another?

For many immigrants, many of those who came to the United States as individuals, seeking fortune meant a better economic life than what had been possible for them in an Old World country. Fortune meant a life with better opportunities for food, housing, health, and wealth than what they had known before. Fortune might be seen as a collection of "things" that could be labeled and noted when they had been found or achieved.

For other immigrants, many of those who came to the United States as families or identifiable groups, the fortune they sought was the preservation of identity that was being taken from them by political oppression or lack of empowerment.

The Scots and Welsh Highlanders of the 18th-century immigration cycle were part of this dynamic.

Their countries had been taken over by the English who were creating "Great Britain" and their long-loved identity was being stolen from them. This also included many Irish residents, many of whom had come there from Scotland and Wales and later moved on to America.

Jack is part of this immigration cycle. He is not looking for money or work or things. Rather, he seeks fortune that is a preservation of the cultural identity that was taken from his forebears in their homelands and that they sought to preserve in coming to this New World.

This culture is to be found in their music, their dance, their food habits and choices, their right to make whiskey, their freedom to practice chosen religion, and their disdain of governmental control. These characteristics may still be found defining much of Scots-Irish-Welsh Appalachian culture even today.

As descendants of those original immigrants, Jack may not know exactly what he is looking for, but he clearly knows what it is not. And, he has a sense that when he finds it, he will feel that he is truly home.

Discussion Questions

1. Jack didn't know what his fortune was, so he made some trades along the way to seeking it. These exchanges may not have looked wise to you. What trades made the least sense to you? Do you think Jack's reasoning justifies his decisions? Explain your reasoning.

2. The dictionary defines "fortune" as chance or luck *or* as a large amount of money. What does "fortune" mean to you? Do you think it means the same thing to everybody? Give an example.

3. How do you think people "seek their fortune" in today's world?

DONALD DAVIS was born in the southern Appalachian Mountains of North Carolina, where he grew up hearing Jack tales and other traditional stories from his Scots and Welsh relatives.

After graduating from Davidson College and Duke Divinity School, Davis served as a United Methodist pastor for 25 years before retiring to tell stories and teach storytelling full-time.

He travels most of the year as a performer and teacher. Davis has authored 18 books, including *Southern Jack Tales* and *Jack and the Animals*. He can be heard on more than 50 audio recordings.

Davis now lives on Ocracoke Island off the coast of North Carolina.

Margarita, La Cucarachita

Adapted by Olga Loya

Once there was a little cockroach named Margarita. Margarita was pretty, but she thought she was ugly. She looked in the mirror and moaned, "Oh, I'm so ugly."

Her mother said, "But Margarita, you are so pretty!"

Margarita looked at her mother sadly and said, "No, I'm not pretty. You just say that because you are my mother!"

All day long, Margarita stood in front of the mirror looking at herself, moaning and groaning about the way she looked, *"No me gusta mi pelo, es demasiado rizado!* I don't like my hair, it's too curly!"

"No me gusta mis pestañas, son tan cortas. I don't like my eyelashes, they are too short."

Then she stuck her lips out and said, *"No me gusta mi boca, es tan pequeña!* I don't like my mouth; it's too small!"

She looked down at her clothes and moaned, *"No me gusta my vestido tampoco.* I don't like my dress either."

Then she groaned, *"Soy tan corta también!* I'm so short, too!"

Margarita was walking along one day thinking about the way she looked when she found a little coin purse with five silver pesos. She knew exactly what she was going to do with that first peso.

She went and bought herself a brand-new wig. It had long, black, straight hair. She loved that wig. Whenever she met someone, she leaned toward them and while she was running her fingers through her hair, she said, *"¿Hola, cómo estás?* Hello, how are you?"

Margarita stood in front of the mirror and said, "I like my wig, but I don't like my eyelashes. They are too short."

So with her second peso she bought herself some false eyelashes. They were sooooooooo long and strong that she could hold a pencil with her eyelashes. Whenever she met anyone, she fluttered her eyelashes and she said, *"Hola,* Hello."

She looked in her mirror and said, "I like my wig and I like my false eyelashes. Then she stuck out her lips and said, "But I don't like my mouth; it is too small."

She used her third peso and bought herself some lipstick. She carefully painted her mouth until it was as big as she wanted. She blotted her lips. After that, when she said good-bye to anyone, she blew kisses toward them and said, *"Adios,* Good-bye."

Margarita looked in the mirror and said, "I like my wig, I like my false eyelashes, and I like my painted mouth. She looked at her clothes in disgust and said, 'But I do not like my dress.'"

She took her fourth peso and bought herself a dress with little birds on it. She liked her dress very much. Whenever she walked, she moved from one side to the other so her dress made a swishing sound as she walked—*swish, swish.*

But she still had a *problema,* problem. She was always moaning, "I am too short!"

With her fifth peso she went and bought some high heels. At first, when she tried to walk on her new shoes she teeter-tottered around, but she finally learned how to walk on them without nearly falling.

She dressed up and looked in the mirror. She had on her wig, her new eyelashes, her new lips and dress and her high heels.

She was walking down the road all dressed up. She saw Señor Gato, Mr. Cat coming toward her.

Señor Gato was *guapo,* handsome. He had beautiful black fur, a long mustache, and mysterious yellow eyes.

He stopped, leaned back and looked at Margarita, and with his eyebrows going up and down he said, *"Meeeeooooow, Margarita, errs tan bonita, porqué no te casas conmigo?* Margarita, you are so pretty! Why don't you marry me?"

Margarita was happy! Señor Gato, Mr. Cat, thought she was pretty! She thought he had beautiful black fur. But then she decided to find out a little bit more about him.

"Y cómo bailará y cantará en nuestra boda? How will you dance and sing at our wedding?" asked Margarita.

"Oh, yo ballaré y cantaré asi, Oh, I will dance and sing like this," said Mr. Cat. He put his paws up in the air and began to dance and sing in loud screeching, *"MMMMMMEEEEOOOOWWWWWW!"*

"No, no," said Margarita. "Even though you have beautiful black fur, I will not marry you! I would be afraid."

Poor Mr. Cat went sadly down the road.

Margarita was feeling good! She had her first proposal. She was walking down the road thinking about Mr. Cat. She thought, Well, he was handsome, but he was so noisy!

Then she saw *Señor Perro,* Mr. Dog, walk toward her. He was *guapo,* handsome, with brown fur, shiny brown eyes, and white, white, teeth. He walked up to Margarita, he leaned back, looked at her from foot to head with his eyebrows going up and down and said in a deep voice, *"Yip, yip, Margarita, errs tan bonita, porqué no te casas conmigo?* Margarita you are so pretty! Why don't you marry me?"

Margarita thought, Well, he does have beautiful eyes. Then she asked, *"Y cómo bailará y cantará en nuestra boda?* How will you dance and sing at our wedding?"

"Oh, yo bailaré y cantaré asi, Oh, I will dance and sing like this," said Mr. Dog. He stretched his arms out to the side and began to dance and sing as he howled loudly, *"AHWOOOOOO!"*

"Nunca, nunca, Never, never!!" said Margarita. "Even though you have beautiful brown eyes, you are too loud. I will not marry you. I would be afraid!"

So poor dog went down the road with his tail between his legs.

Margarita was feeling wonderful! She was walking down the road thinking about cat and dog's proposals when she saw *el Ratoncito,* Little Mouse, He was *also guapo,* with smooth gray fur, a perfect little pointed nose, and a soft black felt hat on his head.

He leaned back and looked at her. Finally he said, *"Squeak, squeak, squeak, Margarita, errs tan bonita, porqué no te casas conmigo?* Margarita, you are so pretty! Why don't you marry me?"

Well, he does have that lovely black hat, she thought. Then she asked, *"Y cómo bailará y cantará en nuestra boda?* How will you dance and sing at our wedding?"

"Oh, yo bailaré y cantaré asi, Oh, I will dance and sing like this," said Little Mouse.

Little Mouse began to sway back and forth and sang in a sweet voice, *"Margarita, eres tan bonita; Margarita, mi amor,* Margarita, you are so pretty. Margarita, my love."

Margarita looked at Little Mouse and smiled and said, *"Si, yo me caso contigo,* Yes, I will marry you."

Margarita and Little Mouse were walking to her house when she suddenly realized, Oh, I cannot keep on my wig, or my false eyelashes, or my painted mouth, or my dress with the little birds, or my high heels. He is going to see me. *Qué hare,* What will I do?

Well, she decided what to do.

When they got to her house, she took el Ratoncito to the kitchen and gave him a nice big cup of coffee.

Then she went into the bathroom. She took off her wig, *shuuu,* she took off her eyelashes, *sh, sh,* she rubbed off her painted mouth, *whoosh.* She left on her dress with little birds and then she took off her high heels, *tock, tock.*

Then she looked at herself in the mirror. She never looked at herself because she did not like the way she looked. As she looked, she was very surprised. Her hair still was curly but was in soft shiny curls. Without her long eyelashes she saw that she had beautiful big brown eyes. She looked at her mouth and saw that it was small but it was perfectly formed. She liked what she saw!

She went out to the kitchen. Was el Ratoncito going to like what he saw?

He looked at her from one side. Then he looked at her from another side. He said, "Come, let us look in the mirror."

As they looked, he said, "Cucarachita, you were pretty before but now you are *bellisima,* beautiful!"

She looked at the mirror, then she looked at him, then she looked at the mirror. She smiled and said, *"Yo se,* I know."

La Cucarachita Margarita never again wore her wig or her false eyelashes or painted her mouth big. But she did continue to wear her dress with the birds. And she always, always wore her high heels.

In time, La Cucarachita Margarita and El Ratoncito were married, and they lived a long and happy life.

Commentary

I first heard a version of this story when I was at a storytelling festival in Guadalajara, Mexico. I came back to the United States and could not remember the story, so I filled it in with my own story. Since that time, this story has gone through many changes, and I think it is finally finished.

When I tell the story, I have the audience put their arms up and make the worst meowing sounds. I have them put their arms to the side and howl as loud as possible. This is especially fun to do in a quiet library.

At the end of the story, I talk to the audience about how we look in the mirror and always wish for something different—oh, I wish my mouth was smaller/bigger; my hair is too straight/curly; I wish I was taller/shorter, etc. I ask them to turn to their neighbor and tell them one thing they like about themselves. Not, "I like my shirt," but "I like the way I look in my shirt."

I chose this story because I think Margarita is a strong character trying to find out about herself. If we have time, I have them share some of the things they like about themselves, and I encourage them to go back to the classroom and share what they like about themselves. I finish this part by saying, "If we can't be kind to ourselves, we can't be kind to someone else."

Resources

Belpré, Pura. *Perez and Martina: A Portorican Folktale.* New York: F. Warne, 1060.

Cuenca, Hector. *La Cucarachita Martina: Adaptación de un Cuento Popular.* New York: Lectorium Publications, 2007.

Deedy, Carmen Agra. *Martina the Beautiful Cockroach: A Cuban Folktale.*
    Atlanta, GA: Peachtree Press, 2007.
Moreton, Daniel, and Miguel Arisa. *La Cucaracha Martina: A Caribbean
    Folktale.* New York: Turtle Books, 1997.

Discussion Questions

1. Many of us, like Martina, find fault with what we see when we look
   in the mirror. It's a good idea to try to see something you *like* at the
   same time! Turn to your neighbor and tell them one thing you like
   about yourself—not, "I like my shirt" but "I like the way I look in my
   shirt." Then listen as your neighbor does the same thing.

2. Now tell your partner something you like about him or her. Listen as
   your partner tells you something he or she likes about you. Being kind
   to yourself is important; sometimes that's easier when others are kind
   to us.

3. You've heard, "Beauty is in the eye of the beholder." What do you think
   that means?

4. Different cultures have different standards of beauty. What is considered beautiful in African American or Latin or Asian cultures may
   be very different from your own personal or familial ideas of beauty.
   What does "beauty" seem to mean in what you've learned from your
   culture?

5. The concept of beauty also changes over time. Do you think there is a
   standard idea of "beauty" in America today? If so, what do you think
   it is? How do you think it looks? How do you think this image affects
   the way people feel about themselves and others, and the way people
   treat one another?

A creative and dramatic mix of Spanish
and English flow together as Latina OLGA
LOYA performs a rich repertoire of family
stories, folktales, myths, historical stories,
and legends. She combines her skills as a
teacher and performer to encourage participants to listen, to use their imagination, to begin to tell their stories, and to
develop a love for the word—for the story.
She has been a featured teller at many festivals including the Guadalajara, Mexico
Festival and the Jonesborough, Tennessee National Storytelling Festival.
Loya performs and teaches storytelling in museums, theaters, conferences,
correctional facilities, universities, libraries, festivals, concerts, and schools
throughout the United States and Mexico. She was the recipient of the
National Storytelling Network's 2013 ORACLE Circle of Excellence Award.

The Tunic of a Happy Man

Retold by Antonio Sacre

Había una vez, y dos son tres, a long, long time ago, at the height of the Umayyad Caliphate, when Spain was not Spain but Arabia, there lived a king and his son in splendid happiness. He ruled justly, and the entire court knew that one day the son would do so, too.

But one morning the prince could not get out of bed. A fever racked his body, and he could eat no food or drink any water. All the doctors and sages of the court were summoned. Each in their love for the prince and the king did their best to cure him, and each failed. The prince sank deeper into sickness, and the king never left his side.

The end was near for the boy, and the king commanded that black drapes be hung in every window of the palace. That afternoon, a strange woman appeared at the gates and presented herself to the court. She seemed ancient in her face and yet strangely strong in her body, and her eyes shone in the darkness of the great hall.

With a low voice that somehow rang throughout the room she called, "I know what will save the boy!"

They rushed her into the room and the king leapt from the side of his son toward her. "Is it true, dear woman, that you can save my son, the delight of my heart, the hope of my days?"

"It is true, your highness. All the prince needs to be healthy again is the tunic of a happy person."

"The tunic of a happy person? Where will I find one?"

"This I cannot tell you. But it has to be from a truly happy man or woman. They must not have one desire or wish. If you were to offer them anything in your kingdom, they would deny it, because they already have everything they could ever want."

"I am king to countless people. My lands are vast. I will not stop until I find such a one. Thank you, dear woman, thank you! What can I give you as thanks?"

"Oh, nothing, your highness."

He looked at her, his eyes wide.

"Are you a happy woman? Is my search already ended!?"

"I wish for nothing except young legs to walk on and a stomach that would allow me to eat sweetmeats again." Her eyes sparkled, the king almost smiled, and she turned and went away.

The king wasted no time in summoning his four chiefs of the guard.

"Go throughout my vast kingdom on the fastest horses in my stable. Find a man or woman who is completely happy. But test them first! They must be truly happy. Offer them in my name their highest wish, anything that I own or can procure for them. If they are not moved by what I can provide, buy their tunic from them, at any price! I will give a fortune in land and gold to anyone that brings me such a tunic!"

Off they raced, those four men, on horses of such speed and strength that it seemed as if the four winds themselves had been unleashed from Odysseus' bag of winds.

One chief flew toward the north and searched every town, every village, every house and hovel, and everyone he asked said they knew of no such person. In the last town at the farthest point, just at the border of the vast kingdom, he approached a rich merchant's house.

Flowers bloomed, fountains burbled, fruit trees provided shade to happy birds, and everything about the manor was peace and contentment. With hope blossoming in his breast, he knocked on the great door, and inside, a gentle man brought him into a sunny courtyard.

"I come from the king on an urgent mission, but first, a question: are you a happy man?"

The merchant smiled and said, "Look at this courtyard. Look at my home! Look at my children and my wife. See how we live! I could not be happier."

"You are completely happy?"

"Of course. God has blessed me with health, wealth, and a loving family. What more could I ask for?"

"The king says that you can have one wish, your greatest wish, and after you tell me what it is, he will ask for one small thing in return."

The man's eyes looked downward and his hands touched lightly at his fingertips. He then rubbed his hands together softly and looked at the chief of the guard.

"Well, I've always wanted a place in the king's court. It wouldn't have to be a big place, maybe fourth or fifth at his table. I could live with sixth, if it were on his right side. Or maybe the prince is looking for a bride? My daughter is passing lovely, and to be married into the king's family would make my happiness complete! Or maybe just a slight increase in my property to the south. I've always wanted to include the forest as part of my own . . ."

Without even waiting for him for him to finish, the chief wrapped his cloak around him, exited the home, and mounted his horse back to the palace. He reported to the king that if a truly happy person were to be found, it would not be in the lands to the north.

The chief of the guard who rode to the east and the chief who rode to the west met with the same result.

The chief of the guard who rode to the south especially loved the young prince, and he vowed never to return until he found what was needed to bring the prince back to health. At first, he met with the same response among the people to the south, and after searching each manor, house, and hovel, he started searching the forests and the fields.

In the last field in the south, where the prairie meets the mountain ranges, he reached the end of the kingdom. He watched the sun turning the mountains and the trees golden, and he felt the fresh air in his lungs. If the prince were not sick, this chief might be the happiest man in the world. He wiped away the tear that fell down his cheek and turned toward the north when he heard a lovely sound . . . a simple, lovely melody from a flute reached his ears, and he turned his horse toward the sound.

There, just at the edge of the mountains, in the shade of a huge elm tree, a young shepherd sat and played a homemade flute while carefully watching his flock.

The guard rode up, dismounted, and sat next to the shepherd. He listened in silence while the young man finished the musical phrase. The shepherd smiled at the guard and offered him a bag of water.

"Are you a happy man?" the guard asked.

The shepherd returned, "Are you?"

"I could be, but the prince is near death, and that weight on my heart makes it impossible to be so. But I repeat, are you happy?"

"My flock has fresh grass. At the base of the mountain is freshwater where we drink and I can swim. I made this flute last month and taught myself how to play! And, I can breathe this fresh mountain air, and every time I breathe, I feel the life that I have. How could I be anything but happy?"

They sat in silence. The chief looked around and felt happiness, too. And then he remembered his mission, and asked, "The king says that you can have one wish, your greatest wish, and after you tell me what it is, he will ask for one small thing in return."

"Any wish? What kindness! What generosity! I have never heard of a king like that. Maybe in the stories of old, but a real king, willing to grant any wish? That is a thing to be sung about, to write a song about . . ."

"Yes, yes, but what is your wish?"

"My wish? Any wish? Did you not understand me? I have everything I need, everything I could ever want."

"This is a once in a lifetime opportunity, and I can give you anything in the world that you desire."

"Anything in the world that I desire? Everything that I desire is right here, right now. This air, this flute, this shade, this mountain, that flock."

The chief waited. The young shepherd picked up his flute again, and before he could play, the chief said, "God be praised, we have found you! A happy man at last, the prince is saved! Please, sell me your tunic, and I will leave you to your happiness and your flock."

"My tunic?"

"Yes, yes, your tunic!"

"I am sorry, I cannot do that."

"Yes, you can, it's an order of the king! Please make this easy for us, for I am authorized to drag you to prison and take it from you by force!"

"You can take me to prison, but you won't be able to take it from me."

"It doesn't have to be this way. Just give it to me. Please."

"What I mean to say is, I don't own a tunic. In the summer I don't need one, and in the winter, all I wear is my wool coat. I've never owned a tunic."

The boy picked up his flute and began to play. The chief smiled, and said, "Will you please come to the palace with me?"

Back at the palace, the king knelt weeping by his son's side. The chief brought the shepherd in, who saw that no words would help.

Sometimes, when words won't help, music can, and the shepherd brought his homemade flute to his lips and played a mournful, beautiful tune. It sounded like the mountains, and the prairie, and the cold mountain air. It sounded like a mountain stream, brisk and inviting. The king looked toward the shepherd, and through his tears, nodded in appreciation.

When he turned his gaze back to his son, he was amazed to see the prince's eyes open and his head slowly turning toward the song.

With parched lips, he spoke, barely audible, "Father! That music reminds me of my childhood, when we would survey our fields and we would eat figs and apricots while walking. If I could eat just a bit of fig, and a bit of apricot . . ."

The chief flew from the room and returned with the fruit, and each day, the shepherd played, and each day, the prince grew stronger, until one day, he sat up in bed and asked the shepherd to teach him how to make and play a flute such as his.

The king leapt for joy and hugged his son, and hugged the shepherd, and hugged his chiefs and his whole court. The feasting began and didn't end for three days and three nights, and after the celebration, the king called for the happiest man in the world, the man who didn't even own a tunic, and he was nowhere to be found. He was back where he wanted to be, and the king vowed to make his kingdom the kind of place where more than only one person was happy, and all people could have a tunic if they wanted one, and if it made them happy, they could choose to not have one, either.

¡Colorín, colorado, este cuenta se ha acabado, y el tuyo ya ha empezado, que sea mas salado!

A Few Quick Notes on the Story

Había una vez, y dos son tres . . . literally means "Once upon a time plus two equals three," but is just a way of saying "Once upon a time in Cuba."

¡Colorín, colorado, este cuenta se ha acabado, y el tuyo ya ha empezado, que sea mas salado! This is a traditional way to end a story in Cuba; it literally means "The color is red, this story has been read, yours is just beginning, I hope that it's saltier than mine!"

The Spanish word in the original story is *túnica,* which means "tunica," which is Latin for "tunic," but refers to the undershirt that people would wear beneath their other garments in olden times. The Calvino story is called "The Happy Man's Shirt." I like "tunic" instead of shirt as it sets the story more firmly in the times it might have been originally told. When I tell it for young children, I just say shirt.

Commentary

I was introduced to this story from one of my absolute favorite books on folktales called *Cuentos que contaban nuestras abuelas: Cuentos populares Hispánicos* by F. Isabel Campoy and Alma Flor Ada.

Many of the folktales in countries where Spanish is the primary language come from Spain. The local populations in the western hemisphere took the bones of the stories, mixed in elements, language, and situations absolutely specific to their own countries, and created new stories.

Not quite 2,000 years ago, the mighty Muslim Empire spread as far west as northern Spain. For 800 years, what was to become Spain and the Muslim Empire had years of war and peace, and both cultures heavily influenced the other in music, food, architecture, and story.

What I love about the "Tunic of a Happy Man" is the mix of the three major cultures and religions: Christianity, Islam, and Judaism. This story probably has its origins with a story of a meeting between Alexander the Great and the Greek philosopher Diogenes. The Muslim Empire acquired the story when it conquered Greece and brought the story through the Middle East to what would become Spain and then back again. The Spaniards then brought it to the lands they were colonizing, and each place kept some of the same elements and changed many others.

In one of the versions I read, the king is a caliphate, the old woman is from the tribe of Israel, and the shepherd is Christian. All three religions (in that version of the story) exist to help one another and heal the wounds of each other by speaking simple truths of love, healing, and forgiveness.

It is powerful to read and hear stories of people working together, even in times of war, to find a cure for what ails the next generation. It shows me that if we cannot have it in reality, we can have it in the imagination, and if anything can help us out of the mess we've created for our children, it's a new imagining of what is possible with reminders from the past. I also love how the story is a melting pot of three major cultures and religions that have much in common, even with all that divides them.

I first read this story before I became a father myself. I was struck by the quiet contentment of the shepherd. I marveled at how he was able to truly be happy with what he had, and it made me stop and think for a moment about my own life. I had health. I could breathe reasonably fresh air. I had the food I needed and a place to sleep. Maybe I was truly happy, too.

No, not at all. There was too much I had to accomplish, too much I wanted to see, too much I wanted to do. That striving may be a part of my DNA, the American-born child of an immigrant father from Cuba who came to the United States with only the shirt on his back. I had much to live up to, much to fight for, much to accomplish.

Now, I am a father of two children, and when I revisited the story after the birth of my second child, I was struck by how much pain I found in the story: what if one of my own children were sick, almost to the point of death?

The example of a father doing whatever it takes to cure his child really hit home for me. And yet, the example of the shepherd is what I want to teach my own children. Be happy with what you have, where you are. Play music when you can. Take care of your responsibilities. Take care of others. Know that the world is not about how fancy your clothes are, or your phone, or your car, or your house, or how far you've made it. It's what you have inside. Learn from others, no matter how high and noble or poor and humble they are. Enjoy nature. Read more. Listen more. Do what you need to do and go back to what makes you happy.

Resources

Andersen, Hans Christian. "The Talisman." In *The Complete Hans Christian Andersen Fairy Tales*. New York: Random House, 1993.

Calvino, Italo. "The Happy Man's Shirt." In *Italian Folktales Selected and Retold by Italo Calvino*. New York: Harcourt, Brace Jovanovich, 1956.

Campoy, F. Isabel, and Alma Flor Ada. *Cuentos que contaban nuestras abuelas: Cuentos populares Hispánicos (Tales Our Abuelitas Told: A Hispanic Folktale Collection)*. New York: Atheneum Books for Young Readers, 2007.

Coloma, Luis, *La Camisa del Hombre Feliz, por el P. Luis Coloma de la Compañía de Jesus, Cuentos para Niños*. Alicante: Virtual Library Miguel de Cervantes, 2000.

Discussion Questions

1. In the story, you heard from various characters about what would make them happy. Do you think these are the same things people value in your community? Why or why not?

2. What do you think is the difference between what people *need* and what they *want*?

3. Reflecting on advertising, news reports, video media (television, streaming channels, films) and social media, what seems to be valued in American culture today (examples: fame, power, money, knowledge, popularity, skills)?

4. What is your definition of happiness? Do you think it changes with age, experiences, or circumstances?

5. Do you think it is ethical to make someone else unhappy to achieve your goals?

ANTONIO SACRE tells stories—for 25 years, in 13 countries, in 45 states, for over 3 million people. His tales of growing up bilingual in a Cuban and Irish American household have inspired children worldwide to gather their own family stories and become storytellers themselves. His stories have been published in award-winning books and audio recordings. His professional development and keynote addresses have helped educators teach writing to students from pre-kindergarten through graduate school. Now his stories are being developed for film and television. He lives in Los Angeles with his wife, two children, and two cats. Yes, he's a cat guy. For more, visit. www.antoniosacre.com.

La Llorona

Crafted by Jasmin Cardenas

Dicen que cuando la luna está llena, They say that when the moon is full, *la noche está negra,* the night is dark, *y el viento canta,* and the wind howls . . . *Pheeeew! . . . pueden ver a alguien buscando por la noche!* You will find her searching in the night, *buscando sus hijos! La Llorona!*

She is known in all the land, in Mexico, Colombia, South and Central America as the Wailing Woman, *La Llorona,* a spirit who is searching for her children. The story is that she murdered them in angry vengeance and immediately regretted her actions, and now she walks the land grabbing other people's children. She is a sort of bogeyman, whom people tell of to scare children into coming home before dark.

There are many stories about her. Like the one *mi abuelita,* my grandmother, told me.

When my abuelita was just a young mother—my mamá was still a *bebé* in her arms, and *mi tío,* my uncle, was a four-year-old—my abuelita spent the day at her own mamá's nearby *ranchito.* She had such a wonderful day there that she didn't want to leave, and it got dark. *Y la noche no es hora para las mujeres en la calle.*

My abuela was worried because in the night she might come across a thief on the road, an animal or a spirit of the night. So she hurried and lifted her son, my tío, on her back, creating a sling with her shawl, *su rebozo,* and carried my mamá, just a baby then, in her arms and said, *"Adios Mamá, Nombre de Dios.* Good-bye, Mother, bless me." My great-grandmother, *mi bis-abuela,* gave her the blessing, *"Que Dios te Bendiga.* God bless you."

And my mamá, a babe in arms, traveled with my abuelita. My grandmother was so worried, it was dark. *Pasó por las praderas,* walking through the prairie, down the hills, and past the streams, she sensed an eeriness about her, as if someone was watching her. *Abuela,* holding her *niño en el espalda* and her bebé in her arms, cautiously walked. As she got closer to her *casa,* she was sure someone was there. As she opened the door to her little house, her *casita,* and turned to close it, she saw . . . her . . . there . . . with *pelo despelucado,* crazy tangled hair . . . *ojos grandes y tristes,* big sad eyes . . . *cara llena de lágrimas,* tear-streaked face . . . *y un vestido en trapos,* and tattered dress.

"Ayyyy!!!! Mis Hijoooooos!!"

She slammed the door. She put the baby down, *"Hijo usted vio eso, esa vieja . . . usted la vio?* Did you see that?"

"Si mamá. Si mamá. Ella estaba agárrando su reboso! She was pulling on your shawl!" cried my uncle. My abuelita got down on her knees and prayed, *"Ángel de mi guarda mi dulce compañía no me desampares ni de noche ni de día. No me dejes sólo que me perdería*—My guardian angel my sweet companion, forsake me not, neither night nor day. Do not leave me alone, I would be lost."

She cried for God, *"Mi Dios!"* to save her and protect her and the babies. And mi abuela never went out at night alone again.

I want you to know something: La Llorona was not always *una vieja,* an old woman, *con pelo despelucado,* with crazy tangled hair, and *ojos grandes y tristes,* big sad eyes, and *cara llena de lágrimas,* tear-streaked face, and, *y, un vestido en trapos,* a tattered dress. No, La Llorona was once a beautiful young woman, the daughter of Don Vicente. Don Vicente was a wealthy landowner in Colombia, and he owned everything as far as the eye could see. There were mountains upon mountains upon mountains that were his land, and Don Vicente had very wealthy friends. On his beautiful plantation, *hacienda,* he had the prize of prizes, the most beautiful young daughter, with long black hair, big emerald green eyes, and a smile from ear to ear, and she wore grand dresses of the finest lace. Her name was Esmeralda. *Esmeralda tenía pelo negro, ojos grandes y verdes, una sonrisa bella y vestidos de encaje.*

Such a prize was Esmeralda that she was promised to the other very wealthy—and very old—landowner from the north. Pero Esmeralda loved her papa, and Esmeralda loved her mamá. She was a very, very obedient daughter. And so Esmeralda knew that one day she would leave her hacienda. But until then she would stand high up on her *balcon* and watch the workers from her balcony.

The workers had very difficult work. There was a *cafetal,* a coffee plantation, *y había muchas platanillas,* and many plantain trees grew, and this work was not for the faint of heart, no. You had to be strong and young. They had long, sharp tools called machetes, and they would climb up the *plataneras,* and— *ta-ta-ta*—cut down the very long *racismos de plátano,* big stalks of plantains. Plantains, if you've never eaten them, are like a cousin to the banana. There are many, many plátanos on a stalk and they are very heavy.

Esmeralda would spend her days watching *los trabajadores,* the workers, and one in particular caught her eye. *Con piel de canela, con ojos grandes y café,* beautiful chocolate skin with big brown eyes, he was so handsome. She didn't know his name, but he noticed that she noticed, that he noticed, that she noticed, and she stood on the balcony fanning herself—it was hot in Colombia!

But she was betrothed so she had never spoken to him. *No lo conocía de nombre, solo de ojo.* She knew him not by name, only by sight.

Once in a while, he brought a rose to the balcony, *pero de vez en cuando el le llevaba una rosa al balcon,* and she would race down to get that rose and hold it tight because she knew it had been gifted to her.

One day *el papá de Esmeraldo* was going to take off to do some business in another faraway area. Her father took some of his workers to attend to business, *y se fueron en caballos,* and they left on horseback. Esmeralda and her mamá stayed in the house, doing what they do, which wasn't much because they were wealthy. And one day she heard, *"toc-toc-toc."*

Are those stones on her *ventana?* Esmeralda opened the window and there he was . . . *el chocolate,* the sun-kissed man.

"Come down, Esmeralda, come down!"

"No, no, no, what will Papá say?"

"Your papa's not home. *Venga.* Come."

"But what will Mamá say?"

"Shh!! *No se preocupe. Venga. Solo vamos hablar.* Don't worry. Come on. Let's just talk."

"Alright, but I can only talk very quickly."

She went down quietly. They spoke.

He was very handsome, and she was very beautiful. They talked about silly things . . . what they liked to eat . . . what they did when they were kids. They would play in el cafetal as if they were little kids running around and under the coffee trees and laughing. Esmeralda had never giggled so much in her life.

Night after night, they would visit and chat. It was oh-so-innocent, and oh-so-beautiful. And her heart felt in a way, *que nunca nunca,* she had never felt before.

One day he said, *"Esmeralda, su papá va regresar."*

"Yes, I know he's going to return. *Y después no vamos a poder vernos.* I know, we will not be able to see each other again."

"*Vamos. Te quiero Esmeralda. Vámonos. Venga conmigo.* Let's go. I love you, Esmeralda, come with me."

"I could never go with you. Papá would never forgive me. Mamá, she would never forgive me."

"Alright, then marry that old man!"

"*Es que yo no lo quiero, yo no me quiero casar con el. Yo quiero estar contigo.* I don't want to marry that old man. I want to be with YOU!"

"Then come with me."

Esmeralda felt like she had to follow her heart. The next day she prepared her things for an escape for a forbidden love that could never be understood, especially not by her *familia,* family. And the next night, with just a comb to brush her beautiful hair and a few small things in a sack, *se salió por las escaleras de atrás.* Down the back stairs she went, and out to el cafetal to meet him.

Then they started to run. They ran all that night. They ran all the next day, *corrieron y corrieron y corrieron.* She knew she would have to run far away, as far as she could, where no one would recognize her, where no one would know that she was the child, the daughter, *la niña, la hija de Don Vicente.*

They ran and they ran and they ran for days, only sleeping for moments. When they got as far as they could by foot, they paid someone to take them on a wagon south as far as they could from the old man in the north and as far as she could get from her father to the east. They got to a town where no one recognized them. They thought they'd be safe.

Back on her hacienda on the first day, no one noticed that Esmeralda was missing because it was the time of the *cosecha.* The harvest was ready, and everyone was very busy. With all the workers rushing about, it was easy to not notice that she was gone. But the very next day her mother noticed. There were many questions and they knocked on Esmeralda's bedroom door.

"*Esmeralda. Despierte está durmiendo mucho.* Wake up from sleeping so much. *Mamita,* you have to get up . . . Esmeralda is gone!"

"Ojo! Ojo!" She called the main workman, the one Father had left in charge. "*Ojo, búscame a mi hija. Búsquela. No la encuentro por ningún lado. Ojo*—Look for my daughter. I can't find her anywhere! Look for her!"

Ojo gathered up the workers and they went out to the coffee fields to look for Esmeralda. Maybe she had gotten lost. Maybe she had fallen and hurt herself. Maybe she was *herida,* wounded. She could've fallen in one of the ravines.

Soon it was clear she was not on the land. She was not in town. No one had seen her. Sure enough, they noticed that one of the workers was missing, too.

"*A buscarlos.* Find them."

Ojo sent word to Esmeralda's father, who was away on business, to return immediately. Ojo went out with the workers to search for her on horseback, *caballo,* with the dogs. They rode for days, they rode for weeks, they returned to the hacienda.

The father said, "*Búscamela YA! Búscamela la nina!* Search for her NOW!"

The search took weeks and weeks, months. They had almost given up hope, *pero al fin un día,* but finally one day, when Esmeralda *estaba lavando su ropa en un río, chu-shu-shu-shu, chu-sh-sh-sh,* was washing her clothes along the river, she heard horses and dogs. Then her love came running.

"Esmeralda! *Corra! Corra!* Run!" Esmeralda saw them coming. They grabbed her love.

She cried, "NO!"

She stood up slowly, for she was large with child. She and her love had married and they were starting a familia. Even though they had just a small shack on the edge of a town, it was all that she loved. And it was hers. When the *caballos* reached her husband, they began to drag him away.

She yelled, *"NO! NO! Déjenlo!* Leave him alone!"

She heard him screech, *"Corra! Corra!"*

Esmeralda took off running as fast as she could, but it wasn't fast enough. His cries stopped. She looked. She couldn't see him fighting anymore. Someone came and grabbed her. They threw her on a horse and returned to la hacienda where her Papá was waiting. He took one look at her, *"Desgraciada.* You are a disgrace to our family."

They threw her into a little locked shack, fed her every day, and her belly grew large. Then, on the day when the pains began, they sent a woman, a midwife to help her. *La partera la ayudo.* The midwife helped her. And after many hours . . . *wah! wah! wah! No había uno, sino que habían dos, gemelos.* Not one baby, but two! Twins!

La partera took care of Esmeralda and cleaned up the babies. And in her rush to leave the shed, the midwife left the door unlocked and rushed to *la casa* to tell Don Vicente that he was a grandfather to twins.

Esmeralda knew this was the only chance that she'd have. Even though she'd just given birth to her babies, she wrapped them up in a cloth and she began to run as fast as her body would take her. She went to the river first because she knew that the dogs would lose the scent. She walked along the river's edge with her babies, brand-new babies. Then Ojo appeared at the other edge of the river and she moved fast, but he moved faster, *"Deme esos crios!* Give me those kids!"

And he tried to pull them away from her. He pulled, and she pulled, and he pulled, and she pulled! *Wah! Wah! Los bebés se cayeron al agua!* The babies fell into the water!

Esmeralda jumped into the river.

"Ay mis hijos! Mis Hijos! MIS HIJOS!!"

She drowned trying to save her babies, *y el coraje que tenía en el corazón no la dejó descansar.* The courage of her heart did not let her rest.

The pain of losing her love and then her children has never allowed her spirit to rest. It has kept her spirit alive all these years, wailing and searching and trying to save her innocent baby twins. *"Ay Mis Hijos!!"*

And that is why they say that if you are out late in the evening, without an adult, you better be careful. She is still weeping. She is still searching. She might mistake you for her own child. Be careful, because La Llorona . . . she might . . . GET YOU!"

Resources

Jaimes, Luis Carlos Valenzuela. *Colombia Mitos y Leyendas.* Bogota, Colombia: Editorial Educativa KingKolar, 2016.

Silva, Fabio. *Mitos y Leyendas Colombianos/Seleccion y Adaptacion.* Santafe de Bogota: Panamericana Editorial, 1999.

Commentary

Telling the Story

For non-Spanish speakers, the story can be read in English only by skipping the italicized words and phrases. I would suggest trying to say La Llorona's (La Yoe-roe-na) weeping wail *"Ay Mis Hijos!!"* in Spanish to keep the authenticity of her voice in your storytelling. The actual translation is "Oh!!! My Children!!! The Spanish translation can be pronounced: *"Eye!!!! Mees-Eee-Hossss!!!"* If possible, try to say it in your highest register, adding breathiness to your delivery and a feeling of pain and eeriness.

At the very end of the personal story that begins this tale, the character *Abuelita* kneels down and prays a prayer in Spanish. Catholics may be familiar with this Daily Prayer to the Guardian Angel:

> Angel of God, my guardian dear,
> To Whom His love commits me here.
> Ever this day be at my side,
> To light and guard, to rule and guide.
> Amen

When I perform this story, I use much less translation in words. I lean into my body, voice, imagination, and timing. To not translate word for word, my bilingual style incorporates creating a rhythmic movement using gestures and repetition to help the audience understand. My experience is that even non-Spanish-speaking children get it.

About Authenticity

The personal story about my grandmother at the top of the story needs a bit of clarification. Colombian readers would note that in Colombia women don't wear *rebozos,* shawls. Rebozos are a very specific traditional, handmade Mexican garment. In Colombia, a shawl is called *un mantón* or *un chal,* but these are not traditionally used to carry children. The grandmother I speak of is my husband's grandmother, and the baby mentioned is not my mother but my mother-in-law. This is her personal tale.

Teresa Nuñez was born in the tiny rancho *La Desiada,* just outside of Moreleon, Guanajuato, Mexico. To simplify the telling, I changed this truth in performance but feel it necessary to give her and her family the credit of its origin.

For years I read many versions of La Llorona, looking to better understand a woman who drowned her children. In the most common versions, La Llorona is a woman who falls in love with a man who leaves her for another woman. Her loss, pain, and feelings of abandonment cause her to lose the will to live, or her desperation turns into fury and rage so she murders her children in an act of vengeance. Sometimes she catches her lover with another woman, and she acts out in a jealous rage. In all the versions I was familiar with, La Llorona acted out violently from a place of overwhelming emotion. She regretted the heinous deed immediately but is unable to undo her actions, and her spirit cannot rest. This is why she walks on the earth wailing and crying, *"Mis Hijos!"* as she searches for her children. It wasn't until I started reading Colombian versions of the story that, surprisingly, I found a more sympathetic character. In some versions, the children die accidentally and sometimes La Llorona tries to save them.

Colombia is the country with the second-highest biodiversity in the world, behind Brazil. Just as diverse as its flora and fauna are Colombia's problems. One example from societal expectations is expressed in this story.

In this version of the story, Esmeralda's father has promised her hand in marriage to an older, wealthy man. Esmeralda rebels and chooses to follow her heart. Her self-determination challenges the patriarchy of her father's plans for her life and how it will benefit his wealth. When she is caught, her father calls her a *Desgraciada de la familia*. To be a disgrace in her father's eyes is to disgrace her proud family, affecting their public image, which is an incredibly painful moment for a girl who lived to please her parents.

Different regions of Colombia offer different versions of her story, and time also affects what is shared. Colombia has a strong Catholic tradition that has brought morality into play with this age-old folktale. A more surprising version I found speaks of La Llorona having an abortion and how she appears to men who dishonor girls, or she appears to frighten girls who have committed acts of which their parents would not be proud. This to me is an example of how religious or political interest can really change a story and why it's so important to seek out different versions and familiarize yourself with the origin story.

La Llorona's origin story begins with the mythological character or deity that predates the Spanish conquest of the Aztec Empire and the colonization of the Americas. Different indigenous groups have different goddesses with similar attributes, one of them is the goddess named *la Cihuacóatl* of the Nahuas. Once the conquistadors arrived and with the spread of colonialism, the legend grew into La Llorona, who is a beautiful indigenous woman who falls in love with a Spaniard.

Esmeralda's actions challenge a very real structure of classicism that still exists in Colombia today. Economically, it is evident in how the neighborhoods are rated *"primer estrato, segundo estrato, quito estrato"*—first strata, second strata, fifth strata. Much like real estate and property taxes work in the United States, neighborhoods are categorized similarly. Unofficially, though, it is regular practice to discriminate against residents of lower strata. This is experienced in questions for job applications, and even access to medical service and educational opportunities.

Colombia is unfortunately known for its machismo. *Merriam-Webster Dictionary* defines *machismo* as a "strong sense of masculine pride." In this version of the story, every male character acts out from his machismo in different moments.

In the story, I mention el cafetal many times. Colombia is known for its *café,* coffee, and my father was born and raised on a coffee farm. The coffee tree grows in the shape of an umbrella with the leaves and beans growing out and down from the center and cascading down like a waterfall. When the coffee tree is fully grown and the harvest is full of leaves and beans, it is easy to hide underneath. I have fond memories of playing hide-and-seek with my brothers and my cousins on our family farm.

Discussion Questions

1. La Llorona lives in the stories passed down from one generation to the next. Do a little family research: Ask members of your family about folktales they might know, and the history or folklore of your family's culture. Ask them to remember stories they heard in school, or from the adults of their childhood, parents, other relatives, neighbors. Ask them about favorite stories from books or other resources. Share your findings.

2. Consider stories you heard growing up, stories from parents, aunts, uncles, or grandparents that might have been told to scare you into listening or behaving in a different way. Note any creepy characters, monsters like the bogeyman, and the descriptions of their appearances and actions. If you did not hear such stories, you may have read them

or seen them in movies. What underlying lessons do you think you were supposed to learn from them?

3. Share anything in the story that surprised you.

4. Esmeralda lived in a different time and place, but you may feel that, in some way, she was similar to you. She wanted to please her parents and did not like to disobey them. We've all felt that way at times. But Esmeralda faced other emotional experiences. How was Esmeralda's life similar or different from the emotional experiences we may have today?

5. Reread the Commentary. Discuss some examples of present-day societal expectations on girls and women in Colombia.

6. Consider a time in your life when you didn't have the freedom to choose. How did this make you feel? How did you react?

7. How do you think you would feel or react if your daughter married someone of a different class, race, or culture? Do you think your response would be based on the best interests for your child, or opinions you've heard or learned or acquired, or in the realities of knowledge and a broad base of experiences?

© Photo by Jazmín Corona

JASMIN CARDENAS is a Colombian American bilingual storyteller, actress, arts educator, and social activist from Chicago, Illinois. Jasmin performs for both children and adults, telling ancient myths, legends, and folktales in her *Cuentos From the Americas* program. In 2016, she performed as an Exchange Place Teller at The National Storytelling Festival in Jonesborough, Tennessee, and has since been a featured teller around the country. A recipient of The RaceBridges Storytelling Fellowship, some of her stories mirror her heart for justice. Jasmin has been a featured storyteller and presenter at the National Storytelling Conference, was interviewed on the podcast Appleseed, and her personal stories can be found on the RaceBridges Studio and 2nd Story podcasts. Jasmin is a professional stage and TV actor, and proud SAG-AFTRA union member who's appeared on NBC's *Chicago Fire, Showtime, The Chi,* and ABC's *Betrayal.* For more, visit www.JasminCardenas.com.

Chango and the Drum

Retold by David Gonzalez

Chango, warrior god and seer of the future, was tending to the people who had traveled from far and wide to hear his predictions for their lives. There were people camped out in his yard and more waiting at his gate. There were people everywhere he could see waiting a turn to peek into their future. And Chango gave each one a throw of the magic seashells. He cast his eye into the scattered shells on the ground and saw the births, marriages, and deaths that awaited them. He saw too their expectant, eager eyes as he threw the shells. He saw how their faces lit up at the good news and how their faces sank and drooped when they heard the bad news. He had the power of the future, with all its ups and downs.

One afternoon, while Chango was in the middle of reading someone's fortune in the shells, he heard the faint beat of a drum. He glanced up and saw that all of the people in his yard were moving to the street. As the beat grew louder, more and more people headed toward it. Even the man who was having his future told left Chango's hut and went out to the street. Chango noticed that a great crowd was assembling around the music, and he too went out.

The music was like a river, clear and churning. It was like a fire, bright and hot. It was like a rock, solid and round. It was like the wind, racing and invisible.

Everywhere he looked he saw people swaying and dancing to the beat of the drum. All the people were happy, smiling, holding each other, and laughing together. Great circles formed around the drummer, and finally Chango saw that the hands that were playing this magical music belonged to Orunla, one of his brother orishas who had lived with him in the land of the Creator. Chango himself was swept into the joyful sound and began to dance with great movements of his arms and legs. He swung his ax above him and twirled with fast leaps and turns. All around him people were dancing with great joy, and Chango saw how powerful the drum was.

Chango asked Orunla to have dinner with him, and when the meal was done and both gods were satisfied, Chango said, "Dear Brother, today I saw the beauty of the drum to bring happiness to the people. I have the power to bring the future to the people, but you have the power to make them forget time all together, the power of joy and community. I would like to propose a trade. I will give you the power of fortune-telling if you would give me the power of the drum."

Orunla had been playing the drums for many, many years and knew that change would be good, and so it was arranged. Ever since that day Chango has the power of the drum and Orunla can see the future.

Commentary

Like many Cubans, my father grew up worshipping a mix of Catholic and African deities. His record collection ranged from big band jazz to mambo to field recordings of sacred ceremonies of the Santeria tradition. Somehow, he was able to make all these different things fit together in his head and heart. In the Yoruba tradition of West Africa, deities are called orishas, and Chango is one of the most powerful. He is the god of thunder, dancing, fire, and drumming. My dad told me this story, and it always makes me wonder what powers are the "true" gifts we have, and what are we willing to give up to get what we really need? In performance, I do a lot of rhythmic vocalizing, mimicking the sound of Chango's beautiful drumming.

Discussion Questions

1. It's said that like Chango and Orunla, everyone has a special talent. What's yours?

2. What talents do you feel are most important and valued in your culture? Why do you think they're considered important?

3. If it were possible to trade talents with someone else, what talent would you be willing to give up, and what would you want in exchange?

Photo by Carl Cox Studios

Storyteller/musician/poet/playwright DAVID GONZALEZ received the Lifetime Achievement award from International Performing Arts for Youth, and was nominated for a Drama Desk Award for his original production of *The Frog Bride* at Broadway's New Victory Theatre. He was named a fellow of the Joseph Campbell Foundation and was the host of *New York Kids* on WNYC for eight seasons. He wrote *Rise for Freedom!,* an opera libretto commissioned and produced by the Cincinnati Opera, and *Mariel,* an Afro-Cuban musical that won the Macy's New Play Prize for Young Audiences. His poetry has been featured at Lincoln Center's Out of Doors Festival, Bill Moyers's documentary *Fooling with Words* on PBS, and NPR's *All Things Considered.* His performance poem, *Oh Hudson,* was commissioned by the Empire State Plaza Performing Arts Center to commemorate the quadricentennial of Henry Hudson's exploration. He is the author of numerous plays and one-man shows that have been presented at many of the best performing arts centers, theaters, and festivals in the United States and abroad. David was a featured performer at the National Storytelling Festival and received his doctorate from New York University's School of Education. Mr. Gonzalez is bilingual and is the artistic director for the Crisalida Communications, a company that consults on arts outreach to theaters and community organizations. For more, see www.davidgonzalez.com.

4

Voices Declaring the Diversity of the African Diaspora

Sukeyna's Journey: A Wolof Tale

Adapted by Charlotte Blake Alston
From the story "Kumba Am Ndey ak Kumba Amul Ndey"

Deysana was not her name. It had become the name she answered to since coming to this place; the name murmured on the tongues of villagers who saw how she was treated. Poor thing. In essence, that was what Deysana meant—"poor thing." This moniker fit the life she led now. It had only been a few months since her mother had left this world. At that moment, the elders had told her, her mother became an ancestor, a love-filled spirit that would always be close.

Her father had remarried shortly after and brought his daughter to live in his new wife's village. This woman had a daughter of her own. Her name was Kumba. Kumba was very spoiled. Whatever she wanted, she got. Her mother would take her to the market and buy beautiful cloth, which she then took to the tailors who would sew the fabric into fine, perfectly fitting clothing. Her mother bought her jewelry for her arms and neck, and oils for her bath. But Deysana—poor thing—if she accompanied them to the market, she had to use the money she was given, money to purchase chickens, meat, or vegetables and spices that would be used to prepare the meals.

Kumba was given money to buy jewelry, cloth, and sweets. When they returned home, Kumba went visiting. Deysana started cooking. In the early morning, Deysana prepared water and oils for Kumba's bath, then began to sweep inside and out. She carried clothes to the river to wash, cooked all the meals, washed all the pots and the bowls, and swept the house clean every day.

But, Deysana's spirit was not broken. She was polite, kind, patient, and respectful. It did not mean she was not sad. She yearned for her mother—for the one who had given her life. And indeed, it was because of her mother that her spirit had not been broken. Her mother had taught her well—even as a very young child.

"Among our people," she would say, *"yaru, yaatu, sutura, muñ*—kindness and respect and openheartedness, patience are most important. They will serve you well in all things."

"Foolish talk!" her stepmother would say.

One day Deysana was looking for a bowl to mix some cooking ingredients. She noticed a dish on a high shelf and reached for it. It was the *mbattu,* the dish used to prepare special foods only on special religious occasions or special celebrations like baby-naming ceremonies. Her stepmother was just entering the house. When she saw Deysana pick up the mbattu, she shrieked! *"Laay laay la laay!* What are you doing?" The sudden, loud, scream startled Deysana. She jumped and dropped the bowl. It shattered into pieces.

"Oh! *Laaye, laay, la laay!* That dish was given to me by my old ancestors! Look what you have done! I knew that you would do something like this! You are a horrible child. You are no good from the inside out." She hit and cut and slashed Deysana with her words.

"You will take my dish to the river Ndéégu Ndaayaan (Nday-goo Ndye-Ann) and fix it or you will never live in peace in this house!"

Poor Deysana. She removed her head covering, picked up the pieces of the bowl, wrapped them in the cloth, and slowly walked out of the house. Ndéégu Ndaayaan. The river was said to have healing power. But very few people who attempted to reach the river ever returned, and those who did were never quite in their right minds again because of all the unimaginable things they had encountered on their journey through the strange and mysterious forest that led to the river. Deysana knew that what her stepmother really wanted was to get rid of her. Deysana asked if she could wait for her father's return from a trip to say good-bye but the stepmother grew increasingly insistent and loud.

"Bu ma la fi gisati!! I don't want to see your face in this house until you have repaired my dish!"

Deysana started walking toward the mysterious forest. She walked and walked, her mind swirling with anxious thoughts. Soon she couldn't see her village anymore. As she walked, she sang softly to herself:

I don't miss sleeping in comfort
I only miss my mother
What I want, no one sells
What I ask for, no one can give

The sun was approaching its highest point when she saw that the trail was leading her right into a forest. She knew this was the mysterious forest everyone spoke of. She didn't know whether to walk faster or slow down.

"Just walk," she whispered to herself, "Just walk." Her mouth was dry. Soon, she came upon a strange sight. A tree, using its branches as arms and hands, was picking its own leaves and fruit and placing them in a pile on the ground. Deysana stopped. She felt her throat tighten, but in an instant, her own mother's words came back to her; *yaaru, yatu, sutura, muñ:* kindness, respect, openheartedness, patience. She had been taught not to show any unusual behavior if she were to encounter a strange spirit but to look and to be calm. She knew this was not a normal tree. Deysana got down on one knee, acknowledged and greeted the spirit in the tree. The tree spoke to her, "You, child, are very respectful and polite. Wherever you are headed in life, you will have God's blessing and protection. Here, take something to eat."

The tree gave Deysana some of its fruit. She ate the fruit. It was sweet and juicy and quenched her thirst. When she was full she continued on her way.

She still had the pieces of the bowl in her hand
She had to get to the river called Ndéégu Ndaayaan.

Her thirst quenched and feeling stronger upon eating the fruit, she left the tree and continued to walk deeper into the mysterious forest, singing softly to herself.

The sun was now lower in the sky. Soon, she came upon a large pot that was cooking its own contents without a fire underneath. She stopped and held her breath. In her head, her mother's words were as clear as a bell: *yaru, yaatu, sutura, muñ*. She showed no surprise on her face. She didn't point or shout. Again, Deysana got down on one knee, acknowledged and greeted the spirit in the pot. The pot spoke to her, "You, child, you are very calm and respectful. Wherever you are headed in life, you will be blessed. Come and eat." The pot gave Deysana a taste of its contents. No stew had ever tasted as good or was as filling. When she was full and satisfied, she continued on her way.

She still had the pieces of the bowl in her hand
She had to get to the river called Ndéégu Ndaayaan.

She continued to walk even deeper into the forest as the path began to be covered with vines and creepers. For the rest of the day, time after time, Deysana encountered one strange thing after another, things so strange that I shall not even try to describe them to you. But for each strange thing she saw, she remained calm and respectful. At each encounter, she was given something that would help her at each part of her journey.

Just before the sky grew completely dark, she could hear the waters of the magical river. She was practically there when she saw the strangest creature leaping toward her. As it got closer, she saw that half the body was that of a forest creature; the other half was the body and form of a wrinkled old woman. She had one eye, one arm, and one leg and could only hop. Thick and matted hair covered both sides of the body, front and back down to her knees. She smelled of rotting fruit. Deysana's mother's words were like loud whispers in her ears: *yaru, yaatu, sutura, muñ*.

Once again, as she had done so many times on this journey, Deysana got down on one knee, acknowledged and greeted the old woman respectfully. The old woman looked amazed.

"You child," she said, "How respectful you are. What are you doing in this place? How did you get so far? And all alone! Tell me your name."

Deysana told the old woman about her stepmother and about the dish. As she spoke, she felt her eyelids getting heavy. The old woman took Deysana home and gave her something to eat. "Now you must go to sleep. I am the Mother of all the creatures in this forest. They all come back home at night to sleep and if they find you here they will not let you live."

She gave Deysana a large metal comb with a sharp, pointed tip and told her to get under the bed. "When my family comes and gets into the bed, you stick them with the comb little by little, *ndank, ndank*. They will think there are ticks and fleas in the bed. They will get up and leave. Then you can get into the bed and sleep in peace."

Sure enough, as soon as Deysana drew in her arms and legs under the bed, the creatures started coming one after another, piling into the bed. Deysana took the pointed end of the comb and, just as she was told, she began to stick it to them little by little, *ndank, ndank*.

Bouki, the hyena, jumped up and said, "Heh! There are a lot of fleas in this bed. We'll never be able to sleep. Let's find a better place." They all left, and

Deysana climbed into the bed. She closed her eyes and slept a deep and peaceful sleep.

In the morning, the old woman led Deysana to the river, took the broken pieces of the bowl, and dipped them into the water. The bowl was restored. The woman wiped it clean and said, "You are a very good child. When you saw how I looked, you didn't show any surprise, you didn't shout, point, or run away. You showed a lot of discretion. And now I am going to give you three eggs." Deysana listened to the instructions carefully with patience and calm.

"When you break this first one I am putting in your hand, a crowd of people will appear. They will follow you and protect you on your journey home. When you are a third of the way, you must break this second one I am putting in your hand. Strange and horrid creatures will come out of it, but do not be alarmed. Then, when you are close to your village, break the third one I am putting in your hand. That will be my gift to you. And this name of yours—it is not a name for one such as you. You are rich in ways that cannot be measured. Claim the name your mother gave to you at birth. Now go. Wherever you are headed, God will be with you."

Sukeyna was her true name. Sukeyna—one who will always return.

She now held the restored bowl in her hand
She had made it to the river called Ndéégu Ndaayaan.

Sukeyna thanked the old woman and left. She walked quickly, holding the mbattu close to her body. When she could no longer see the old woman's dwelling, and was a third of the way home, she broke the first egg as instructed. A large crowd of people appeared and began to follow her. When she had traveled another third of the way, she broke the second egg. And just as the old woman had said, strange and vile creatures arose, but the crowd of people surrounded them and destroyed them, every one. When she was close enough to the village to smell the food cooking in the pots, she broke the third egg. The mbattu dish began to overflow with gold. She removed her head cloth and emptied the precious jewels into it. She tied it into bundle and walked into the village.

She came into the house, greeted her astonished stepmother, and said, "Here is your bowl. I have restored it as you asked." For a long moment the woman was speechless and stunned. How could this child be standing in front of her once again? And where could she have found these treasures?

She called her own daughter. "Kumba! You must come here at once!"

She grabbed the bowl from Sukeyna's hands, and just as Kumba entered the house, she tossed the bowl to the floor. "Look my daughter! My special bowl is broken! You must take these pieces to the river Ndéégu Ndaayaan and restore it!"

Kumba looked back and forth from the broken pieces to Sukeyna's bundle overflowing with treasures. "Oh! Yes!" She eagerly picked up the pieces and said, "Yes, yes, I will go and restore this dish."

Kumba picked up the pieces, ran quickly out of the door and walked briskly onto the trail that led into the mysterious forest. Soon, she came upon the tree that was taking down its own leaves and fruit. "Hoo-ooh!" she yelled in surprise. "What is this? A tree taking its own fruit down! This is crazy." Kumba didn't wait for the tree to offer her anything. She went toward the tree and grabbed a piece of fruit and began to eat as she continued on her way.

The tree called after her. "You there, child. How rude and disrespectful you are. You are not going to get very far."

"I may not get far, but I got what I want and that is some fruit!" But the more she chewed, the more bitter the taste and soon, she was spitting it out.

She left the tree and continued walking deeper into the forest.

She came upon the pot that was cooking its own contents with no fire underneath.

"Oh, are my eyes deceiving me? What madness is this? This cannot be real!" But the smells of the pot's contents teased her hungry stomach! She took one of the broken pieces of the dish, dipped it into the pot, and ate and ate and ate. The stew was most certainly real and most certainly delicious she thought. She continued on her way.

"You there, girl," the pot called after her, "You are not very wise. You will not get very far."

"I may not get far, but I got what I want and that is some stew." But after a few more steps, her stomach felt completely empty.

With each encounter, Kumba pointed and laughed, clapped, exclaimed, and grabbed whatever suited her. But she was growing restless and impatient.

As the sun was setting, she came upon the old woman.

She squinted her eyes and held her nose and shouted. "Old woman! When did you last bathe? What are you doing out here? You should be hiding yourself!"

"You there, child. You don't show a lot of discretion. You are not a wise or thoughtful girl. What are you doing here in my forest?"

"I am here to restore this dish, so just tell me where I need to go!"

"Even you cannot find your way in the darkness. You will sleep, then I will take you in the morning."

She took Kumba to her house, offered her nothing to eat but told her, "I am the Mother of all the creatures in this forest. They all come home at night to sleep. And as with Deysana, the old woman gave Kumba a large metal comb with a sharp, pointed tip and told her to get under the bed. "When my family comes and gets into the bed, you stick them with the comb little by little, *ndank, ndank*. They will think there are fleas in the bed and they'll leave. Then you can get into the bed and sleep."

No sooner had she tucked in her arms and legs than one after another after another, the creatures piled onto the bed.

Kumba was startled but also so impatient to get into the bed and sleep that she jabbed the creatures with the comb. They jumped up and scrambled on top of one another to escape the sharp jabs.

Bouki the hyena said, "Hey! These are not fleas. We need to see what is under this bed."

Quickly the old woman said, "I will take care of it. You leave tonight and when you come back tomorrow, you will be able to sleep in peace. I promise you." They may have been terrible creatures, but they still always listened to their mother.

The creatures got up and left, and Kumba got into the bed.

The old woman woke Kumba early. She took her to the river and restored the bowl. "You almost caused trouble for yourself last night. You must leave this forest as quickly as you can and never come back."

"I don't need to come back. The bowl is restored. Now tell me where you keep the treasures you gave to the first girl who came."

"I give to you what I gave to her. What you do with them is what you do."

She gave Kumba the first egg and began to tell her exactly what to do. She was about to place the second egg in Kumba's hand, but before she could, Kumba snatched it and ran.

She ran and ran until she was halfway through this forest. At that point, she stopped, looked at the first egg. "A crowd of people to follow me. I don't need a crowd of people.

They'll only want my riches, which I claim now." Instead of breaking the first egg, she broke the second. Vile and menacing creatures sprang up from that egg, and before Kumba could react, they pounced on her. They scattered into all parts of this forest and into the air, and all that was left of this girl was her tongue.

In the village, a group of women awaited her return. Her mother had gathered friends to welcome Kumba back and to see the riches her daughter would bring. They were gathered in the courtyard eating and celebrating. A large bird flew out of the forest, circled over them, and dropped Kumba's tongue in the mother's lap. She screamed, ran into that forest, and never returned. As for Sukeyna, the riches that were passed to her from her mother—*yaru, yaatu, sutura, muñ*—carried her far in her life. She lived the rest of her days in happiness and peace.

Today in cities, villages, and towns; in houses and courtyards; school classrooms and playgrounds; around warm fires in the evenings, people of Senegal gather to hear the retelling of this story. When the children hear it, they are reminded once again of how rich they truly are.

A child that's patient and polite
Who is respectful and shows discretion
Will find honor and fame and be welcomed wherever they go.

Commentary

This story was shared with me when I first visited the country of Senegal in 1988. It's entitled "Kumba am Ndey ak Kumba Amul Ndey (Kumba with a Mother and Kumba without a Mother)." In the traditional version each girl is named Kumba and is referenced in the story as such: "Kumba am Ndey did 'x'; or Kumba Amul Ndey said 'y.'" The story was included in a publication for Peace Corps workers to help familiarize them with the people, the language, their customs, and their stories. The story was written in the Wolof language. The Wolof are the largest ethnic group in Senegal, and their language is the primary indigenous language in the Senegambia region. I was given the gist of the story and told that it was one of the "signature" stories of the Wolof people. Back home in Philadelphia, I was able to connect with a Wolof-speaking, Senegalese student attending the University of Pennsylvania, who translated the story line by line. Completely familiar with the story, he added contextual comments, underscoring why the story had such importance. The story underscored specific values inherent in Senegalese culture, values children were expected to internalize and manifest. These values were also regarded as important tools that children could call upon when faced with challenges as they grew to adulthood. In a sense, the story represents initiation or transition into adulthood—a transition that can be navigated safely and successfully if these tools are harnessed. It also offers a window into the people's beliefs about how stepchildren—or orphaned children—should be treated.

My first and subsequent visits to the Democratic Republic of Senegal remain among the most memorable experiences of my life. Contrary to the media's consistently negative, stereotypical, and misleading information about the African continent, its 54 independent nations, its ethnic groups, and most especially its *people,* the Senegalese are open, warm, and welcoming. Although it is an ethnically, linguistically, and religiously diverse country, the majority of its citizens are practicing Sunni Muslims. The Wolof are the largest ethnic group. Family is a high priority, as is a giving spirit, and one is considered wealthy if surrounded by family and friends. As the Senegalese proverb says: "What you give to others bears fruit for yourself."

Discussion Questions

1. Write down and discuss your initial thoughts about this story. What do you believe are the essential takeaways? Are there aspects of the story you connected to on a personal level? What were they?

2. Make a list of beliefs you have about the African continent and its people. Brainstorm, write, and discuss at least four ways this story reveals information about the people who created it and passed it down. How does the list of your beliefs compare with what the story reveals? How do they differ? How are they similar?

3. Senegal is one of 54 separate and independent countries on the continent of Africa. Can you find the country of Senegal on a map? Identify one or two countries on completely different parts of the continent. Do a little research about each. What are the similarities and differences in each (ethnic groups, languages, national flag, landmass, natural resources, etc.)?

4. In the United States, English is the primary language and the only language most Americans speak. Can you identify three languages that are spoken in Senegal? What would be the advantages of knowing how to speak more than one language?

5. Talk about a time you had to face a challenge or make a decision without your parents or other adults to tell you what to do. Did you learn lessons from your family or community that you were able to apply successfully? If you have not yet had to face such a challenge, what tools have you been taught that you can apply to help you successfully navigate life's challenges?

6. If you had the power to create your own village or community, what are the values you believe would be important to pass to the residents— especially the children? Explain.

Photo by Annie Tiberio

CHARLOTTE BLAKE ALSTON is a nationally acclaimed storyteller, narrator, librettist, and singer who performs in venues throughout North America and abroad. The 2018–2019 season marked her 25th as the host of Sound All Around, the Philadelphia Orchestra's preschool concerts. For 19 years, she was the featured host, storyteller, and narrator on the Carnegie Hall Family and School Concert series. She has made multiple appearances at the Smithsonian Institution, the Kennedy Center for the Performing Arts, the National Storytelling Festival, the National Black Storytelling Festival, and numerous festivals around the country and abroad. She has shared stories in several countries including Senegal, Ghana, South Africa, Japan, China, Ireland, Switzerland, and Brazil. She collaborates with musicians, vocalists, and choreographers. As a librettist, her choral works incorporate storytelling: spoken and sung. Her narrative voice can be heard on a series of health training videos for GlobalHealthMedia.org.

Yelling without Being Loud

By Rex Ellis

Raymond L. Redcross (1911–1996)

(with an accompanying folktale by Lyn Ford)

In the small town of Williamsburg, Virginia, located in the Upper Tidewater area of southeastern Virginia, lived a man for all seasons named Raymond L. Redcross. He was a businessman, mechanic, and church man, a talented organist and a man of few words. He was a respected member of the black and white community, and he loved his family and his Harley Davidson motorcycle. He rode that motorcycle with friends for over 40 years.

Though he was not an educated man, Raymond successfully ran an automotive repair business for many years. Because he was a businessman, he was required to manage his relationships with the black and white community with the skill of a ballet dancer with one foot *en pointe*.

Raymond's philosophy of life was to try and love everybody—even those who dismissed, marginalized, and sought to belittle him. Never sinking to their level, he was nevertheless courageous and forthright, always a gentleman in defending himself when he felt he was being disrespected. His courage "under fire" and his willingness to stand toe-to-toe with those who sought to abuse him were extraordinary.

This story is one Raymond told me about an incident he had with a Virginia state trooper.

The story takes place in the early 1960s, when America was reeling from the end of segregation and preparing for what would be the long struggle of the civil rights movement.

Don't just read the lines of the story, read *between* the lines. Contained therein is the wisdom of Solomon.

There was trouble between the races during that time, but as far as I was concerned—of course I may be a little different from many others—but I made it my business to be able to get along with anybody. If a man, black or white, proved to me that he was a man, then he'd be okay with me. I tried to conduct myself so that I would appeal to him. I never went around with a chip on my shoulder, daring someone to knock it off or saying things I knew would offend this other person. I tried to be a man and respect him as a man.

Sometimes you'd run across one that . . . well, you find them in both races . . . that are not men as far as morals and so forth . . . but I always tried to make it my business to fall in line with that person and win him over if I could. If there was something he did that I didn't particularly like, I'd try to win him. And I have had some that were pretty harsh in the other race.

Once I did have a problem with a state trooper, that was relating to my business. For years I ran a garage. We repaired cars and did general service. I was also doing state inspections during that time. Mine was the only black-owned garage in my area doing inspections at the time. And this particular fellow tried to disqualify me, if he could. The day that he approached me, he did make me quite angry. But I held my temper.

At that time, I had a cinder-block building, but I hadn't painted it. I hadn't gotten around to that because I was trying to get a little more finance. He looked at it and told me I had to "get some paint on this building."

I said, "Well, I had planned to get it painted, I've already secured someone to do it for me, but I hadn't gotten around to it."

He made the statement that, "You'd better have it done by next Thursday. If not, I'm going to turn your name in to the police department." I told him that I was going to do the best I could. He returned—it was not Thursday; he returned that Monday before the Thursday. And he jumped me again, wanting to know why I hadn't gotten the building painted.

"I'm going to do this and I'm going to do that," the trooper said, and so on. I didn't say anything to him, except that I was going to do the best I could. He gave me a certain period of time to get it done.

When he came back the next time, I told him that I'd like to have a word with him. The first times he came, he came alone. But this time he had two persons with him, one was a policeman and the other was a civilian. I told him I'd like to have a word with him.

He said, "What do you want to tell me?"

I said, "I'm not going to do like you did. You spoke to me out in the public. Even the neighbors could hear what you were saying. I don't want to do that; I want to get with you privately where I can say what I want to say to you. Not to the neighbors and the general public. Won't you come in?"

I had a little place in the back where I wrote my tickets and bills for customers—I called it my "little office." He looked at me sort of weird-like, as though I was going to do something to him or something. He looked at his other friends that were with him, the other trooper and civilian, and he looked at them and he looked at me; he looked at them and he looked at me.

I told him, "Come on in, I'm not going to hurt you. Come on, let's go inside."

The other fellows said, "Come on, we'll go along with you."

So all three came in. I said, "I didn't appreciate what you said the other day when you were here. You said something that fretted me quite a bit, made me quite angry. But I'm not going to talk to you like you talked to me. I'm going to talk to you as a man. When you came in that day, I was standing at the door. You came in, and walked all through my shop, looked all under the benches and behind the cabinets and so on. I didn't know what you were looking for, and I didn't know who you were."

He said, "You knew I was a policeman, didn't you?"

I said, "Yeah, you had on your uniform, but a lot of times other people wear uniforms too. I have heard of instances like that, that they wear a uniform but they're somebody else. You didn't say anything."

He said, "I just thought the uniform would tell you who I was."

I said, "Well it didn't. It showed me that it was a police officer, but it didn't show me the man that was in it, and I didn't know who you were."

I said, "I've come in contact with many other policemen and they were just as nice as could be. They asked me questions and they more or less came to help me. They would tell me what to do and what not to do; be careful about this and be careful about that. We got along just like hand and glove. But you, you're altogether different. And I didn't understand that, and I didn't like it."

So, he said, "Do you want to write a letter in on me?"

I said, "No, I'm not going to write a letter in on you because the people up there in Richmond, in the police department, are just as nice as can be. I don't have any problem with them. I've been up there and talked with them; I've worked with them, and they've worked with me, and I've worked with them . . . no problem. But I don't understand you. You didn't act like a man at all. You acted like a hillbilly. . . . I just don't know *how* you acted."

He had his head hanging down by this time. He said, "You angry with me?"

I said, "No, I'm not angry with you." At the time, I felt like I could bite his head off, but I said. "No, I'm not angry at'all, and I'm not going to write a letter in on you. I just had something to say to you. You told me the other day what you wanted to tell me, and today I decided I'd wait until I got a little more ease, and I figured I could say what I wanted to say to you without making myself look bad. And I wanted to tell you that."

He said "Well, I'm sorry I did that. I'm sorry I talked to you like that. . . . I shouldn't have done that." And he had some kind of explanation—something had happened somewhere else the day he spoke that way to me. But he said, "As far as I'm concerned, we're good friends. And if you say you're not angry with me, can we shake on that?"

I said, "Yeah sure we can shake." So, we shook hands, and I shook hands with the other two gentlemen that were with him, and we all smiled, and they left.

I met up with him several times on the highway and he was one of the best state troopers, to me, that I know of in this vicinity. I don't believe he would have given me a ticket unless I had done something real bad. He was just that nice. I remember one time we were on our way to Richmond. I used to ride a motorcycle quite a bit at that time. We were stopped up there near Camp Peary on the outskirts of Williamsburg. It was about 10 or 12 of us. State troopers had stopped us, and were asking for driver's permits, registration cards, and so on. So, I always ride at the tail end of the group. Never in the front or middle. I like to get on the back end. There were three or four policemen coming on down the line checking us. So, it just so happened that this trooper I had talked with that day came to check me. So, I had my permit and my registration out to show. When he got to me, he recognized me.

He said, "Oh, this you, Redcross!"

I said, "Yeah, I'm out here too."

He said, "I didn't know you rode a motorcycle."

I said, "Yeah, I get out here with the boys sometimes, too."

He said, "Oh, I don't need to see your operator's license."

I said, "Yeah, look at mine, too. You looked at all the rest, go ahead and take a look."

I said, "You stopped all of us here, and I'm riding an old motorcycle. . . . The other boys have self-starters, later models. They run better and they look better. Mine doesn't start as easy as some of the others. . . . You may have to give me a push!"

He said, "Yeah, yeah, I'll give you a push."

"Okay," I said, "I'm ready to go." So he got behind and began to push. He must have pushed me about 50 yards. . . . I could have started it sooner, but I didn't. Finally, I put it in gear and we went on.

He yelled, "Alright, boys, you all have a good time."

He was one of the finest police officers on the force.

Commentary

A story from a community member, told to me by one of our church members about his early years (1960s) as an African American small business owner in Williamsburg, Virginia. He is truly a man who learned the art of "yelling without being loud."

A Tale of Cat and Rat

An African American folktale retold by Lyn Ford

Cat had made himself a fine reputation among the rats in the city. They knew him as the best rat catcher that had ever lived, which was bad news for them. So the rats who hadn't yet become cat food moved from the city's dark alleys to the safer, greener countryside.

Soon, Cat found himself desperate for a meal. He moved to the country, too. For a while, Cat feasted on birds and mice, but he had to work harder for those meals. The fields were much wider than any alley, and the critters were quicker than his old prey. Cat missed those tasty rats.

One morning, Cat saw one of them scurrying into a hole in the wall of an old barn. He had an idea. Cat settled himself beside the hole, with his eyes closed and his front paws curled under his chest. Cat stayed there, still and silent, except for a gentle *"purr purr purr . . ."*

Soon a rat stuck her head through the hole, saw Cat, and drew her head back into the barn.

Cat sniffed, sounded as though he were about to cry. But he was really smelling the possibility of a good breakfast. Cat called to the rat, "Sister Rat, please don't run away. I'm so happy to find you and your family!

"I've missed you and all your family, and I've just been sitting here praying you all ignore my past and accept my forgiveness for eating up your kinfolk. Come out here and rest peacefully beside me. Come and visit with me."

From inside the barn, Rat hollered to Cat, "Now, how can you expect me to rest with you? You've been the enemy of my race since cats had teeth and rats had tails. If I dare to visit you, you'll do to me just as you've done to my kin."

Cat yowled and howled, "Oh, I've been mean, I've been bad, and I've been hungry. But I'm sitting here with my paws folded in prayer. Can't you forgive me and be friendly?"

Cat stayed still and silent again, except for that *"purr purr purr . . ."*

Rat was surprised, but she told the other rats what Cat had said. They debated the situation for quite a while. And, all that while, Cat simply sat: *"Purr, purr, purr . . ."*

The rats decided to test Cat's words. Rat slipped out of the hole in the barn wall. She got close to Cat and watched him purr. She got a little closer, and a little closer. And Cat twitched just a little. One eye slightly opened. One paw slowly slid from under Cat's chest, and toward his breakfast, then . . .

Rat skittered, lickety-split, back inside the hole!

Cat pitifully meowed, "Oh, Rat, I thought we were going to be friends!"

"We *were* going to be friends," Rat replied from the safety of the barn, "but I can tell you're still *Cat*.

"So, we rats'll be 'friends' who remember how cats have treated us. We'll be friends who remember the past. We'll be friends who know cats haven't changed much. And we'll stay alive!"

That's the way it was then. That's the way it is now. And cats and rats won't rest peacefully together, side by side, until the day the cats start treating rats the way they treat other cats.

Discussion Questions

1. What does "read between the lines" mean to you?
2. What hidden emotions or responses did you discover underlying the situations, conversations, and comments in Ellis's story?

3. Share your definition of friendship. Keeping your definition in mind, were Mr. Redcross and the Virginia state trooper "friends"?

4. Compare the story of Mr. Redcross and the state trooper with the folktale of cat and rat. State the similarities or differences between them.

5. How does the ending of "Cat and Rat" relate to some newsworthy, present-day incident? What acts of real respect might improve the relationship between those involved?

Dr. REX M. ELLIS recently retired from his position as Associate Director for Curatorial Affairs at the National Museum of African American History and Culture (NMAAHC) at the Smithsonian Institution. Dr. Ellis was charged with planning, developing, directing, and managing collections, exhibitions, publications, and scholarly initiatives for the museum. Curatorial Affairs is the primary implementing office of the museum's mission. In this regard, the office develops preserves, documents, interprets, and makes accessible to diverse audiences the scholarship and resources of the museum through exhibitions, education, and public programs.

He has memberships in the Screen Actors Guild, the American Alliance of Museums, the American Association for State and Local History, the National Association of Black Storytellers, and the National Storytelling Association.

He has been a storyteller for over 30 years.

Contests: Tales of Competition and Determination

Retold by Lyn Ford

Eagle and Sparrow

From the multicultural African American, or "Affrilachian," stories in Edward Cooper's heritage.

Eagle was big, strong, fierce, frightening, and a fine figure of a bird. He declared himself king of the sky, and none of the other birds dared to argue with him. None, except for Sparrow.

"Maybe other birds would like to be king," Sparrow pouted. "Maybe *I* would like to be the queen of the sky!"

Eagle laughed at Sparrow's words, but he noticed that, in whispers and twitters, other birds were beginning to question his authority. Then Eagle had an idea to shame the little bird and impress the others.

"Little bird," Eagle said to Sparrow, "I challenge you to a race. The first one of us to reach the highest point on the highest mountain near here will prove that *he* has the strength and power to rule. The one whose feet touch the ground there first wins. We will race at sunrise!"

The next morning, the birds gathered to watch the race. There in the valley, where Eagle and Sparrow stood side by side in a clearing, the other birds settled in the branches of trees and bushes and waited for the race to begin. As soon as the first ray of sunlight touched the tops of the trees, Eagle screeched, "GO!" Eagle's great wings opened. He rose higher and higher, with the wind lifting him and his strength and speed pushing him forward. Occasionally, he looked to his left and his right, he looked beneath himself and above himself, and he didn't see Sparrow. And Sparrow was definitely not in front of him, which made Eagle laugh. Of course, he thought, Sparrow is behind me, and she is losing this race.

The mountain seemed to come closer and closer to Eagle. He was glad, for he was growing tired. Finally, he lifted his wings to land on the top of the mountain.

From under his wing, dropped Sparrow. Her tiny feet touched the top of the mountain first. Sparrow won the race!

The other birds heard Eagle call out in a rage, "Sparrow, you could not have beaten me here! You could not have flown here before me!"

Sparrow cheerfully said, "I didn't. I hitched a ride with you. You didn't say we had to fly to this spot. You said the one who reached it, the one whose feet touched the ground here first, would win. I won!

"You may have strong and powerful wings, but I have a strength and power, too. It's called a brain, and I know how to use it!"

Sparrow, now the queen of the sky, quickly flew away from there. She could see how angry Eagle was, and she wanted to be safe more than she wanted to be queen. And since then, eagles chase, catch, and eat little birds. So, little birds tend to gather together for safety, and often hide themselves in the branches of bushes and trees.

Yet, you hear the little birds chirping in those branches as they carry on deep discussions and ask thoughtful questions. They are gathering strength and power, asking Queen Sparrow for advice.

Commentary

This is a story of unevenly matched competitors, a tale wherein a creature who is in power because of physical strength, attributes, or abilities unfairly competes against a creature who is smaller, slower, weaker, but always wiser—brawn or bullying versus brains, and brains always win. Better known variants of such tales usually include two protagonists, Tortoise and Hare or Turtle and Rabbit.

For comparison, read the following tale.

The Tortoise and the Hare

Aesopic fable variant retold by Lyn Ford

The Hare always boasted of his speed to all the other animals. "I challenge anyone who would dare to race with me, for I have never been beaten," said the Hare.

And the Tortoise said, "I accept your challenge." Hare laughed, until he heard Tortoise say, "And I challenge you."

When Tortoise challenged him, Hare agreed to the race. The two agreed on the course of the race, and when it would begin. And when the race was started, Hare whizzed forward and out of sight; then he stopped, thinking that he was so far ahead, he could take a nap.

Hare rested under a tree and was soon asleep. As he slept, Tortoise trudged and lumbered on and on, passing the sleeping Hare and reaching the finish line first.

Moral: "Slow but steady progress wins the race."

The morals were not specifically stated in the oldest versions of fables, which made them good prompts for moral discussion.

Resources for a Similar Story

Clouston, William Alexander. *Popular Tales and Fictions: Their Migrations and Transformations,* vol. 1, pp. 266–67. Edinburgh and London: William Blackwood and Sons, 1887.

Jacobs, Joseph. *The Fables of Aesop.* London and New York: Macmillan and Company, 1894, 1902, no. 68, pp. 162–63.

Now, consider a variant whose roots are within the storytelling of several cultures from the continent of Africa.

Turtle and Rabbit

African American Appalachian (Affrilachian)
variant (from Lyn Ford's family stories)

Rabbit bragged about his racing skills and teased other critters because they couldn't run like a rabbit. He made everybody in the woods miserable.

Turtle had a plan to stop Rabbit's bragging. Turtle said, "Rabbit, you and I will race down the footpath tomorrow. If I win, you have to stop bragging and teasing."

Rabbit laughed and said, "You won't win. I will! And when I do, you have to leave this neck of the woods, because I don't ever want to see you again!"

Critters waited at the starting line and the finish line. The birds twittered to start the race. And Big Boss Lion, who was the judge, waited at the finish line to declare the winner. When the race started, Rabbit zipped away from the starting line, and down the footpath through the woods.

And, after a while, Rabbit saw Turtle strolling ahead of him past a big rock! Rabbit ran faster. He passed Turtle, *WHOOSH!*

Much to his surprise, near a blackberry bush just ahead of him was Turtle! Rabbit ran faster that he had ever run, until he was too tired to breathe, *"Huh, huh, huh. . . ."* But he was near the finish line, and he thought he was winning the race. Rabbit set himself down under a tree, and took himself a nap.

Then Rabbit heard critters cheering and laughing, shouting, "Yes! Turtle won!"

"Turtle won?!?" Rabbit cried, and he jumped up from his nap and shot like a streak of lightning toward the finish line.

Then Rabbit stopped. He saw somebody on the other side of the finish line.

You know who it was? That's right, it was Turtle! Around him, animals cheered and shouted as Big Boss Lion roared, "Turtle WINS!"

Rabbit pouted a while, then he hopped home. And Rabbit never bragged or teased again. Some folks say rabbits hide themselves and seldom make a sound because they are still embarrassed about that race. If that one who lost the race had stuck around a little while, he might have seen something and learned something more.

Turtle walked up the footpath. At the blackberry bush, he met Sis Turtle. They walked to the big rock; there they met Mama Turtle. At the starting line, they met Grandpa Turtle. Rabbit didn't know that everybody in the Turtle family looked the same, and they knew that unity is strength.

Turtle, with his family's help, won the race, and that was the end of it. That's the end of this story, too.

Moral: Unity is strength.

Resources for a Similar Story

Fairytales of the World. fairytalesoftheworld.com/quick-reads/the-hare-and-the-tortoise-somalia
Nassau, Robert H. *Where Animals Talk: West African Folklore Tales.* London: Duckworth and Company, 1914, pp. 95–98.

Commentary

Stories were never merely entertainment in my family. They were conduits for education and information, and often combined elements from the diverse storytelling traditions within our heritage. We are Affrilachians.

In the 19th century, the term *Melungeon*, describing people of mixed African, European, and Native American ancestry, was used in Virginia, Tennessee, and North Carolina. I never used that word, nor did anyone else in my family, but others occasionally called us that, when they weren't calling us other names, crueler things. I refer to myself as "Affrilachian," a term Kentucky poet and professor Frank X Walker created; Walker coined this term for African American Appalachians, many of whom include and embrace both European and Native American ancestry in their heritage. "Affrilachian" also reflects the concept of being an outsider in what has long been considered an "outsider" community, the people of Appalachian ancestry.

Stereotyped as poor, ignorant, uneducated, filthy, often lazy, and prone to criminal offenses (moonshining, drunken acts, stealing, and so many more), people of Appalachian heritage have fought against the opinions and actions of societal and financial giants for centuries. Even as some exploit natural resources (coal, oil, wood) and artistic craftsmanship (instruments, music stylings and ballads, quilts, ironworks, and furniture), the beauty of the hearts and minds and the diversity of the region were ignored. Things are changing, slowly, as our families reclaim and carry on their traditions, but we still suffer from the stereotypes and lack of respect for our stories that have been a part of the larger story of America for centuries.

We are still the sparrows attacked by eagles. We still strive to be recognized and respected. And we can be just as cunning when we must. Family unity, the supportive gathering together and listening to those who bear wisdom, is important, too, for unity is strength.

Sparrows tend to build their nests in low places, the branches of bushes, the grassy and weedy areas where they can disguise both themselves and their homes through natural camouflage. One such bird, the chirping sparrow, even hides her call, for her call sounds like the chirping of a grasshopper. In West Virginia at certain times of the year, the eastern golden eagle threatens chirping sparrow survival. These eagles winter in Appalachia.

Discussion Questions

1. Some might call Sparrow's action "cunning." Others might consider it "trickery." In light of the story and the actions of Eagle, develop and discuss your opinion about what Sparrow did. What elements of the story support your opinion?

2. Compare the story of "Eagle and Sparrow" with the two tales, "Tortoise and Hare" and "Turtle and Rabbit." How is each story similar? How is each story different?

3. In the news of our times, what comparisons can you make to the story of "Eagle and Sparrow"? Is there any contemporary situation for which "Eagle and Sparrow" could be a metaphor? How and why?

Adachi: A Dilemma Tale

By Karen "Queen Nur" Abdul-Malik
(with an accompanying folktale by Lyn Ford)

Adachi sprang up from her Friday afternoon nap. She fluffed up her pillows just like Aunt Dara showed her. Adachi checked to make sure that the bedspread was even on both sides, because Aunt Tayibah said, "A well-made bed makes for sweet dreams." Then Adachi took her little hand and made the crease just as neat as Aunt Rere's doily-fied dresser.

She pulled open her weekend drawer. For a minute she could not remember which one of the three distinct piles she was to pack. "That's right, it's Aunt Rere's weekend."

You see, Adachi had lost her mother when she was just nine years old. But her three aunts promised her father that they would help to raise the child. So on the first, second, and third Friday of each month, one sister would pick up Adachi for the weekend.

This weekend it was Aunt Rere's turn. So, Adachi knew it was the first pile. She popped open the gold button on her black patent-leather pocketbook and inspected the white gloves to make sure there were no smudges on the tips. She skipped to her closet and pulled out the personalized suitcase that Aunt Rere had bought for her just last Christmas. She packed her crinoline and the dress with the flowers embroidered at the hem. "Oh, I can't forget my hat?" Aunt Rere was one of the best dressers at the First Baptist Church, and she always topped it off with just the right crown. When the preacher got to praying and the organ got to playing, well, Aunt Rere's hat would start a'swaying as the tambourines sanctified the sound.

Fo'ty days fo'ty nights
When de rain kept a-fallin',
De wicked clumbd de tree,
An' for help kept a-callin',
For they heard de waters wailin'
Didn't it rain, rain
Didn't it rain,
Tell me Noah, didn't it rain?

Some clim'd de mountain,
Some clim'd de hill,
Some started sailin'
An' a-rowin' wid a will;
Some tried swimmin'
An' I guess they're swimmin' still,
For they heard de waters roarin'
Didn't it rain, rain, didn't it rain,

Tell me Noah, didn' it rain,
Didn' it rain?

Mmmm mm mmmmmm mmmm, mmmm mm mmmmm mmmm.

"Adachi, You ready?" "Yes, Aunt Rere, I'll be right down."
The next Friday's visit was with Aunt Dara. Adachi went to the third pile. Very carefully she picked up the beaded bag, the one her mother used to carry

when she wore her special *Ewu*. Aunt Dara was her mother's *ibedji* (twin). In the Yoruba tradition, twins wear the same sacred beaded outfits. Gingerly, she packed the bag with her *lapa* (top), and *gele* (scarf). She was so excited because this weekend was the New Year: the time to throw out the old yams and bring in the new. Adachi would sit at the feet of the *Babaaláwo* (priest) when he told stories about Olodumare, the creator of all things, even the orishas like Yemaya of the ocean; Oya the one who comes like a whirlwind for transformation; Obatala of the white cloth; Ogun, the iron maker; and even Egun, the trickster. Her eyes popped wide, when the rhythm of drums and *shekere* would lead the songs.

> *Ishe Oluwa, Kole ba je ooo.* (God's work can never be undone.)
> *Ishe Oluwa, Kole ba je oo.* (God's work can never be undone.)
> *Kole ba je oo* (can never be undone)
> *Kole ba je oo* (can never be undone)
> *Ishe Oluwa, Kole ba je oo.* (God's work can never be undone.)

> *Omwa bi fi fay shay kole da ru rro.* (What you do with love cannot go
>   wrong.)
> *Kole da ru ro* (Cannot go wrong)
> *Kole da ru ro* Cannot go wrong)
> *Omwa bi fi fay shay kole da ru ro.* (What you do with love cannot go
>   wrong.)

> *"Ecaro Adachi! Bawo Ni?"*
> *"Dada ni,* Aunt Dara. I'm coming!"

On the third Friday, before Adachi heard, *"As salaam Alaikum,* (peace be unto you)," she packed her pink scarf to wear to the Masjid (mosque) because it went perfectly with the *jilbab* (dress) that Aunt Tayibah brought back from hajj.

"Labbaik Allah humma labbaik. Labbaik la sharika laka labbaik. Innal hamda. Wan-ni'mata. Laka walmulk. Laa sharika lak. Ni'mata. Laka walmulk. Laa sharika lak. (O my Lord, here I am at Your service, here I am. There is no partner with You. Here I am. Truly the praise and the provisions are Yours, and so is the dominion and sovereignty. There is no partner with You.)"

Aunt Tayibah shared stories about hajj, and how everyone from all over the world said the same prayer, in the same language, standing, prostrating, kneeling at the same time. And when told how they all circled the first house built to God, by Abraham, Adachi would pretend that she too was in the sea of white going round and round the black Kaaba and walking from the hills of Safa to Marwa like Hagar desperately searching for water for her son. There, so tightly packed that arms and legs seemed to disappear into a flowing white sea, that itself might spring up at the Well of Zamzam.

"Adachi, it was on Mt. Arafat that I kept the promise to make *duas* (prayers) for all the people back home. After reading the prayers they wrote, I closed my journal and opened the Quran. The page fell open to, ". . . With Him are the keys of the unseen, the treasures that none knoweth but he. He knoweth what ever there is on the earth and in the sea. Not a leaf doth fall but with His knowledge."

Just then, silent tears would flow from Aunt Tayibah's eyes. Adachi's lashes too would catch sweet dew.

"My darling girl, I closed the Quran, open my palms, and one single leaf fell in my hand."

"As-Salaam Alaikum, Adachi."

"Wa Laikum As salaam Auntie, I'm all packed."

Yes, Adachi enjoyed the first, second, and third Fridays, but the fourth was her favorite. Her aunts would come to her home. Aunt Dara would bring *fufu*. Aunt Rere perfected the jollof rice, and Aunt Tayibah sweetened the gathering with Akara bean cake. Adachi, her father, and her aunts laughed and shared stories about her mother and aunts' childhood days in Egba, Nigeria. Sentimental fingers grazed the photograph book.

"Yes, look at your mother, our dear Kehinde. There she is in her green and yellow African lace and gold *gele* (crown) for her *Ekun Iyawo*. Oh yes, the cry of the bride. Just like our ceremony back at home . . . what a beautiful song she sang honoring our mother before she left our home to go to her new husband."

"And there I am!"

"Yes, in your grand *Agbada* (clothing)." They laughed between whispers of longing tears. Yes, the fourth Friday was Adachi's favorite.

This is a dilemma tale. Adachi was raised by her father and three aunts, one was Christian, one Muslim, and one practicing the Yoruba religion. When Adachi grew up, what was she?

Translations/Definitions

Arabic

"*As-Salaam Alaikum*—Peace be unto you."
Zamzam—Continual flowing well located at Masjid al-Haram in Mecca that appeared when Hajar was looking for water for her son, Isma'il.
kaaba—Small building in the court of the Great Mosque at Mecca.

Pidgin—Mix of two or more languages from West Africa

lapa—Skirt.

Yoruba

agbada—Four-piece male attire.
"*Bawo ni*—How are you?"
"*Dada ni*—I am well."
"*Ecaro*—Good afternoon."
ewu—Beaded gowns for twins.
fufu—Doughy West African food of boiled and ground plantain, yam, or cassava, made into balls to go with soups or stews.
gele—Scarf.
shekere—West African percussion instrument made from a dried gourd with beads or cowries woven into a net covering the gourd.

Wolof

jollof rice—Dish originates in the Senegambian region.

Commentary

This dilemma tale was created by Karen Abdul-Malik (© 2000). The story is a tale of folk who practice three different religions within the same family structure. The folklife and traditions within the story depict various languages, clothing aesthetics, songs, food, and religious belief systems, yet there is a shared foundation of ethos, values, and morals. Hidden in the

answer to the question posed (When Adachi grew up, what was she?) is con-
sideration of the meaning in the names of the characters. A little bit of
research will reveal that secret.

The three songs in the story are traditional. "O Didn't It Rain" originated as a Negro spiritual and was first composed to sheet music in 1910 by
Harry Thacker Burleigh. "Ise Oluwa" was composed in Nigeria in the early
19th century by an unknown author. The Talbiyah is a prayer that originated during the time of the Prophet Muhammad (570 CE–June 8, 632 CE)
on the road to Mecca for hajj. All songs are public domain.

Leopard* and Anansi's Daughters

A dilemma tale retold by Lyn Ford

Because they were both beautiful and kind and sweet, Anansi's twin
daughters were both deeply loved by Leopard. He wanted to marry one of them,
but he couldn't choose between them.

This bothered Leopard so much that it stayed on his mind day and night.
He didn't sleep, he refused to eat, he forgot about getting anything to drink. For
more than a week, Leopard lived on love and a single thought: Which wonderful woman should he ask to be his bride?

Leopard grew thinner and thinner, weaker and weaker. He fell to the ground
in his own yard and was still. His heart stopped beating. His eyes closed. Leopard took his last breath and died.

Some of Leopard's servants called out for help. Others quickly made their
way to Anansi's house. The twin sisters were brought to Leopard. And when
the older twin saw her potential husband lying lifeless on the ground, she
wrapped her arms around his neck and she died, too.

The younger twin ran home and prepared a medicine so powerful it could
revive the dead. She hurried back to Leopard and poured the medicine all over
him. Some of it touched her sister. Both Leopard and the older sister lived again!

Leopard's servants told him about the way one sister, out of love for him,
died, and the other sister, out of love, brought him back to life. And Leopard
knew he still could not choose between them.

Which one do you think loved Leopard more? Which one of the sisters
would you choose for your partner?

Discussion Questions

1. Discuss the dilemma question: When Adachi grew up, what was she?

2. What in the story reflects the communities where you live or the envi-
   ronments where you work, learn, and play?

3. Discuss how many identities a single person can have and how it may
   impact their view on diversity and inclusion.

---

* This story's roots are among the tales of Anansi the Spider in the Akan (Twi/Fante)
language of the Ashanti people of Ghana. The stories, one of the only things enslaved
Africans could carry and keep with them across the Atlantic Ocean between the
16th and 19th centuries, found new homes in the Americas. In Jamaica, the character Leopard, or Lion, often became Tiger. I've returned the character from "Tiger and
Anancy" stories I heard as a child to his West African persona as Leopard.

4. Dilemma tales are a typically African form of short story whose ending is either open to conjecture or is morally ambiguous, allowing the audience to comment or speculate upon the correct solution to the problem posed in the tale. A dilemma tale nurtures skills in filtering, processing, and critical thinking about the outcomes of actions and scenarios. It also helps those who hear or read the tale to look at their own lives as creative acts in which they have the power to choose or create what happens next. Consider a time when you had to make a choice between two or more actions or items. What choice did you make? How do you think you came to a conclusion about what you should do or get?

5. Because each of the aunts seems to love the girl in this story, it might not seem like a dilemma tale. But, in the end, she must take charge of the choice she makes. What factors do you think might help her to make this decision?

6. This story does not preach or try to force a belief system on the girl. Yet, to practice any one belief system, she might have to give up something. When you choose between two or more best options, what process do you use to make your choice? Do you list the pros and cons, discuss matters with others, do your own research, refuse to make a decision and let things happen? Discuss ways to make choices when either decision seems to be of equal value in your culture.

Queen Nur is the mother of three, grandmother of five. She is an award-winning national storyteller, teaching artist, and folklorist with a master's in Cultural Sustainability from Goucher College. She is the folklife director at Perkins Center for the Arts and executive director of In FACT, Inc.: Innovative Solutions through Folk Art, Culture and Tradition. She has performed and presented in over 30 U.S. states, Canada, and Ghana. In 2018, Queen was Young Audiences of New Jersey and Eastern Pennsylvania Teaching Artist of the Year and New Jersey Governor Awardee. She is the 14th president of the National Association of Black Storytellers. For more, see www.queennur.com.

Anansi and the Magic Cauldron:
An Ashanti Tale

Retold by Bobby Norfolk

Near the town of Kumasi, the rains had refused to fall for several weeks in the spring and summer. The ground became very parched and arid. Big cracks formed in the soil, and the lakes and rivers dried to a trickle. The livestock and wild animals could find no food or water, and they became thinner and thinner and thinner until they all fell over dead—*plop!*—hooves in the air!

Now, Anansi had a wife named Aso, and his eldest son was named Tikuma. One day Anansi called a family meeting. Everyone sat gathered together in antic- ipation of what Kwaku Anansi was going to say.

"We have no food in the house," Anansi stated.

Tikuma retorted snarkily, "Yeah, tell us something we don't know, Baba!"

"Be quiet, Boy, when I speak!" Anansi bellowed.

Tikuma just shrugged his shoulders, rolled his eyes, and looked away.

"Here is what we need," Anansi proclaimed. "Aso, my wife, go north look- ing for food. Tikuma, you head south. I will cover the east and the west. Let's meet back here in two hours and report on findings of food."

Everyone departed and in two hours, everyone returned to report that not a bit of food was to be found. Anansi had gone west, but not as far east as he had intended because he ran out of time. That night, the only things on the din- ner plates were fried bugs, worms, and inner tree bark.

Tikuma got very insulting with his father: "You're supposed to be so brave and have such magical powers! Why can't you find us some food, Man?"

Anansi glared at this son.

"You talking to me, Boy? How dare you talk to me like that?" But Anansi knew the boy was correct—and that he was not in his right mind because of the hunger in his stomach.

Then Anansi remembered that he had run out of time before he had gone as far east as he had intended, so the next morning he went to the kitchen cup- board and got a glass cup and poured a libation of prayer wine to take to the Sacred Grove in the east.

Upon reaching that sacred spot, Anansi poured the libation on the ground, knelt, and said, "Oh Great Spirit, you are full with wisdom and understanding. Help your son find food and water. I ask this, Oh Great Spirit of the Forest." Then Anansi arose and walked slowly back through the forest.

When he arrived at a clearing in the forest, there sat a huge black cauldron. Anansi gawked!

"Whoa! What's that?"

Anansi crept up to the cauldron and gingerly looked in, hoping that perhaps it was full of soup or stew. The cauldron was cold and empty.

In bitter disappointment, Kwaku Anansi moaned, "I wonder who left an empty pot in the middle of the forest? Empty, when I'm so-o-o-o hungry? They must have had a great feast!"

He rocked the pot around, saying, "Maybe it has a name or inscription on it and I can take it back to its proper owner."

As soon as the words left his lips, Anansi heard a voice, coming from the pot. "MY NAME IS DO WHAT YOU CAN DO."

Anansi was amazed—a talking pot! Anansi sputtered, "And what are you able to do?"

The cauldron retorted, "Well, try me and see."

Anansi stood back against a palm tree and said, "Well, do what you are able to do!"

Immediately, there was a pop, and food from all over the world covered the ground! There were couscous, baked yams, cassava, grilled goat and lamb, then spaghetti and meatballs, mac and cheese, hot wings, burritos and tacos, palak paneer, vegetable samosas and nan, Szechuan vegetables with tofu and brown rice, turkey and dressing, cranberry sauce, croissants and quiche, larded beef tenderloin, filet mignon, prime rib, baby back ribs, collard greens, cornbread, and sweet potato pie.

Anansi shouted, "It must be suppertime!"

He ate and stuffed food in his pockets. He ate and ate and ate, until—*burp!*—could eat no more, and still food sat all over the ground in front of Anansi.

He said, "I will take some of this food back to my family." But then, greed set in.

"I don't want them to have all the best food—I'll keep the best food for myself." He separated all of the food that he preferred, putting aside the scraps for his family. Then he built a sled of bamboo and twine. He put all the food he liked on one side, and the undesirable food on the other side. When that task was complete, he reached for the cauldron.

"DO NOT TAKE ME FROM THE FOREST, ANANSI," said the cauldron. "COME AND VISIT ME WHENEVER YOU WISH, BUT IF YOU TAKE ME FROM THE FOREST, YOU WILL BE IN BIG TROUBLE."

Anansi was indignant.

"Shut up, pot! Don't tell me what to do!" Anansi slapped the cauldron with the flat of his hand, then after disrespecting the pot, he put it on the sled and began dragging it home. Halfway back he stopped.

"I don't want the family or neighbors to know about this cauldron," he thought, so he hid it along with the food he desired in a clump of bushes and took the scraps of food that he didn't like back to the family. When he arrived, he kicked open the door—*bam!*

"Aso, my wife; Tikuma, my son—all my children! Come and see what your clever father has brought home!"

The family shouted, "Dad has brought us food!" They dove into the scraps and leftovers, devouring the food eagerly.

While the family was feasting, Tikuma asked, "Father, would you like some food also?"

Anansi stammered, "No, no. I don't desire food. My only joy is to see you happy." Anansi suppressed a big belch.

While the family was engaged in eating, Anansi crept back outside and built a small hut out of bamboo and twine, then hid the cauldron inside. He put a lock on the door of the hut before he went back inside. After that, whenever he was home alone, Anansi would go out to the hut, unlock the door, pull the cauldron out, and demand, "Do what you are able to do!"

On command, the cauldron would produce food from around the world. Anansi would eat all the best food himself, giving the scraps and leftovers to his family. He gave none to friends and neighbors.

One day, when Anansi went to the hut and hauled the pot out, he noticed that it was dusty and dirty. Kwaku Anansi took out palm nut oil to clean it with, but before he began, the cauldron said, "ANANSI, WHATEVER YOU DO, NEVER COME NEAR ME WITH THE SEEDS OF PALM NUTS, AND ABOVE ALL, NEVER TOUCH ME WITH THE OIL OF PALM KERNELS."

Anansi replied, "Excuse me? Don't tell me what to do!" Then he slapped the pot with the flat of his hand. He had disrespected the pot twice.

Anansi got tired of going all the way out to the hut every day and dragging food back to his family, so one day while no one was home, he got a ladder and hid the cauldron in the thatch roof of his house. Every day, when the family went out to work in the fields and forest, Anansi would get his ladder and climb to the top rung, open the thatch, and whisper, "Do what you are able to do."

On command, the cauldron would produce food from all over the world. Then Anansi would crawl under the thatch, eat all the best food, and take the leftovers down for his family. Never did he eat in front of the family.

One day, Tikuma went to his mother in private and said, "Mom, is it not strange that Father always refuses food when we eat—but look how big that man is becoming! What is that all about?"

His mother said, "Ahh, my son, indeed you have inherited your father's wisdom. We know he loves to keep secrets, so don't question things, just let it go."

Tikuma said no more, but he still watched his father as closely as he could, thinking, How is he getting so big not to be eating any food? Surely, he can't be getting big off of breathing air! Did he become a breath-a-tarian?"

Meanwhile, Anansi's thoughts kept returning to the words of the pot. "Why did that pot say don't touch it with the oil of palm kernels?"

Suddenly, Anansi thought he understood. "I know! The pot can produce diamonds and gold and doesn't want me to become rich!" Anansi began to make a plan.

One day when he was dining alone, he found some seeds of palm nuts at the bottom of his soup bowl.

"Well, look here! Ha!" He put them in his pocket and later told the family to go to the Sacred Grove to pray for more food.

As soon as the family was out of sight, Anansi got his ladder and climbed to the top rung, opened the thatch, took the seeds out of his pocket, and said, "Look what I have!"

The pot did not reply.

Anansi laughed. "You do not want me to touch you with these seeds because you can produce diamonds and gold. Is that not correct?"

The pot still did not reply.

Anansi gleefully touched the seeds against the pot.

POP!

Smoke filled the air, and when it cleared, the cauldron was gone. Anansi had disrespected it three times. In its place was a long shepherd's cane. Anansi's eyes bulged out.

"What in the world? Who are you and what can you do? Where did the pot go?"

The cane said, "I am the Avenger, and what I do is just and righteous. Try me and see."

Anansi said suspiciously, "And what if I don't like what you're doing? What can I tell you to do to stop?"

"Don't worry about that, my son, just try me and see," replied the cane.

"Alright, then cane, or Avenger, do what you are able to do!"

Immediately, the cane rose into the air and began to pummel and whack on Anansi. Anansi jumped from the ladder yelling and tried to escape, but the cane chased him through the forest, beating and walloping Anansi on every part of his body.

Anansi yelled and screamed, "Owww! Stop, stop!" The faster he ran, the harder he was struck.

His friends and neighbors heard his wails.

"Anansi is in trouble. Let's go help!" But when they saw the cane doing its work, they backed away.

Anansi's family ran to the sound of his screams and saw what was happening.

"My husband," cried Aso, "what is going on?"

Tikuma, however, had the courage of a young lion. He ran forward and shouted, "Cane! Cane! I know my father is greedy and secretive, but we do love him. What can I tell you to do to stop?"

The cane replied, "Well, you say, 'Calm down.'"

Tikuma shouted, "Calm down! Calm down! Calm down!"

The cane stopped its work, hovered in the air for three seconds, then fell to the ground, once again an inanimate object.

By now, Anansi had welts and bruises all over his body. All of his friends and neighbors came out of hiding and began rubbernecking and wondering aloud about the spectacle.

"Let's go see what happened to Anansi." "He got beaten by a shepherd's cane." "Who was wielding the cane?" "Why?"

As Aso was dressing his wounds, Anansi looked up and saw everyone staring at him. He heard what they were saying, and he decided that they deserved answers.

"I have a confession to make," said Anansi. "I have taken a cauldron from the Sacred Grove that produced food enough for the entire village. I ate all the best foods myself. To my family, I gave leftovers; to my friends and neighbors I gave nothing. And now, because of my greed and selfishness, the cauldron that produced food has been destroyed.

"I want all my friends, neighbors, and children to know: Never be greedy and selfish. Share with other people what you may have. Because if you don't, punishment will be your reward."

And that's the end of that.

Commentary

From the villages of Ghana, West Africa, the timeless tales of Anansi the Spider arose. He is the demigod, the trickster, who teaches from his negative example. In essence, his stories teach us "how not to act." He delights the young and the young at heart by showing us that the importance of human traits such as teamwork and cooperation, respect, honesty, humanity, and compassion can be realized by listening to his exploits.

Carl Gustav Jung, Swiss psychiatrist, immortalized the basis of human personality through the term *archetypes*. All aspects of human activity on a cognitive level are delineated on the archetypal level: king, queen, witch, wizard, fool, trickster, hero, heroine, giant, wise person. Anansi is the trickster, who by his nature guides us to a higher way of interacting with our human neighbors.

These stories left the shores of West Africa on slave ships centuries ago and found their way to the Americas and the Caribbean islands. Unable to bring any material goods on those terrifying journeys, enslaved people brought something even more valuable: they brought their culture, their beliefs and values, their humor, and humanity with them in the form of these stories that have been passed down through the generations.

In the summer of 1993, I visited the country of Ghana, West Africa. I spent a week in the capital city, Accra, and the tour took us to the inner regions of the countryside. One day city officials in Kumasi hosted us. Of the 35 people on the tour, I was the only storyteller. In the question-and-answer period between city officials and the rest of us, I was compelled to ask, "What is the importance of Anansi the Spider in your culture?"

Immediately a woman on the panel broke into a wide smile and said, "Ahhh, Anansi, him Spider—the antihero. Every day when I was a young girl, at 4:30 we stopped what we were doing and the families in the village had 'Anansi Time'!"

Discussion Questions

1. Anansi the Spider teaches by *negative example*—what do you think that means? How would you say Anansi did that in this story? What lessons do you think he taught?

2. The lessons in a folktale represent values that are important to the culture from which they come. Why do you think the lessons in this story were important to the Ashanti people?

3. How can you learn from a negative example? Discuss ways in which you learned from a negative example in your life.

4. We each learn best in different ways. Which do you think is more effective—a negative or positive example? How do you think this applies to the way you learn at home, in school, or with your friends?

5. When the story ends, Anansi's family and the people of the village are left with no magic cauldron and a continued famine. What do you predict will happen next? How do you think they will treat Anansi? Do you think the cauldron could reappear to someone else who is more giving than Anansi? How might that character's story compare with Anansi's experience?

6. What are your definitions of compassion and forgiveness? How do you think these qualities play—or *should* play—a role in this story?

BOBBY NORFOLK is an internationally known story performer and teaching artist. This three-time Emmy Award winner, multiple Parents' Choice Gold and Silver Awards winner, and Storytelling ORACLE Award recipient is one of the most popular and dynamic story educators in America today!

The faculty of the University of Missouri-St. Louis and the Board of Curators voted to confer upon Bobby Norfolk the degree of Doctor of Humane Letters honoris causa. Bobby also gave the commencement speech at the graduation ceremony.

Ole Sis Goose

As told by Diane Ferlatte

This is a literal transcription of Diane Ferlatte's telling of Ole Sis Goose at the National Storytelling Festival in Jonesborough, Tennessee, recorded by Lashon Daley, PhD candidate, Performance Studies, University of California at Berkeley, California.

DIANE. One glorious morning, there was Sis Goose sailing on the lake. Sun shining, not a ripple in the water. It was a beautiful day. And there she was. She was flappin', and kickin', and dippin', flappin', and kickin', and dippin', flappin', and kickin', and . . .

AUDIENCE. Dippin'.

DIANE. Flappin', and kickin', and . . .

AUDIENCE. Dippin'.

DIANE. Flappin', and kickin', and . . .

AUDIENCE. Dippin'.

DIANE. Oh, she was having a wonderful time. But there hidin' in the weeds, in the weeds was guess who?

AUDIENCE. Br'er Rabbit.

DIANE. Br'er Fox. And Br'er Fox said, "Look at her swimmin' on that lake like she own it. I'll fix her." And he waited. And he laid low. He laid low just like Br'er Rabbit. And there she came kickin' and swimmin', you know, dippin'. And when she came close to the bank, Ole Br'er Fox jumped up and caught her.

He said, "Oh, hahaha. I got you now Sis Goose, swimmin' on that lake like you own it, haha but I got you now. And I'm gonna break your neck and pick every one of your bones."

And Sis Goose said, "Hol' up hooooo no, huh, Br'er Fox. Before you go breaking necks and picking bones, no huh, I got just as much right to walk down that street with my ice tea and Skittles without someone followin' me, oh wrong story"!*

Audience laughs and claps.

DIANE. I got just as much right to swim in that lake as you have to hide in them weeds, nah, you don't own this lake. I got just as much right. Now before you get to breakin' my neck and pickin' my bones, we gonna take this matter to the court.

And Br'er Fox said, "Fine, let's take it to the court."

And all the way to the court, Sis Goose was just fussin': "Break my neck. I don't think so, not today, uh, huh, break my bones, uh huh, we gonna see 'bout this. Take this to the court."

Audience laughs.

---

* Reference to Trayvon Martin episode.

DIANE. And she go to the court. When she got to the court, the sheriff standin' at the do' was a fox.

Audience laughs mildly.

DIANE. When she went into the court room, the prosecuting attorney was a fox.

Audience laughs lightly.

DIANE. The defense attorney was a fox. The judge was a fox.

Audience laughs lightly.

DIANE. Everybody in the jury box was a . . .
AUDIENCE. Fox.
DIANE. Mmmhmmm!

Audience laughs.

DIANE. And do I have to tell y'all what happened?

Audience mumbles responses.

DIANE. Huh?!
AUDIENCE. Yes!
DIANE. They tried Ole Sis Goose and they convicted her. And they broke her neck and picked every one of her bones clean. So listen to me good, when everybody in the courtroom is foxes, they ain't gonna be no justice for a poor goose. You want justice? Just look in America's jails. That's just what you'll find, just us.

Audience groans.

Diane sings.

Come and go with me to that land
Come and go with me to that land
Come and go with me to that land
Where I'm bound
Where I'm bound
Come and go with me to that land
Come and go with me to that land
Come and go with me to that land
Where I'm bound
And they'll be justice in that land
They'll be justice in that land
They'll be justice in that land
Where I'm bound
Where I'm bound
They'll be justice in that land

They'll be justice in that land
They'll be justice in that land
Where I'm bound

Ole Sis Goose

Original

Tales of Br'er Rabbit, Sis Goose, and other African American animal stories were originally published in dialectic form devised to represent a Deep South African American dialect. This is the "original" version of the story.

Ole Sis Goose wus er-sailin' on de lake, and ole Br'er Fox wus hid in de weeds. By um by Ole Sis Goose swum up close to der bank and ole Br'er Fox lept out an cotched her.

"O yes, Ole Sis Goose, I'se got yer now, you'se been er-sailin' on mer lake a long time, en I'se got yer now. I'se gwine to break yer neck en pick yer bones."

"Hole on der', Br'er Fox, hole on, I'se got jes' as much right to swim in der lake as you has ter lie in der weeds. Hit's des' as much my lake es hit is yours, and we is gwine to take dis matter to der cotehouse and see is you has any right to break my neck and pick my bones."

An so dey went to cote, and when dey got dere, de sheriff, he was er fox, en de judge, he was er fox, and der tourneys, dey was foxes, en all de jurymens, dey was foxes, too.

En dey tried Ole Sis Goose, en dey 'victed her and dey 'scuted her, and dey picked her bones.

Now, my chillums, listen to me, when all de folks in de cotehouse is foxes, and you is des' er common goose, der ain't gwine to be much justice for you pore cullud folks.

Resources

Botkin, B. A., ed. *A Treasury of American Folklore*. New York: Crown Publishers, 1944.

Eddins, A. W. "Brazos Bottom Philosophy," edited by J. Frank Dobie, Texas Folk-Lore Society, no. II, 1923, pp. 50–51.

Hughes, Langston, and Arna Bontemps, eds. *The Book of Negro Folklore*. New York: Dodd, Meade, & Company, 1983.

Commentary

Many folktales maintain relevance for centuries because their message promotes a lesson, value, or moral considered to be so universal that it can withstand the test of time. Other folktales, such as "Ole Sis Goose," relate to a specific cultural setting, place, and time. This particular tale reflects a specific condition of black folk in America. Since this tale was published in the early 20th century, it has existed in folklore for at least a hundred years and represents how African Americans felt about their place in society at that time. Initially this was a tale told only within the black (Negro) community. The question is, Why is this tale still so popular and relevant today? What does it say about "the more things change, the more they stay the same"?

Discussion Questions

1. How is this story reflective of people's actual experiences a hundred years ago and today?
2. Do you think the foxes realize that they are all foxes with all the power and privilege? If not, why?
3. What would justice look like for Sis Goose today?
4. Are there places today, like the lake, where one group feels it okay to exclude another group? Give examples.
5. In the democracy we live in today, do you feel that we all have equal access to justice?
6. The "original" story variant was an attempt to preserve the unique voice of an African American storyteller, speaking to family and friends, in an era without easy access to recording devices. Can you recognize differences in the way you speak to your friends and family and the way you speak and write in the classroom?

Storyteller DIANE FERLATTE is a multi-award-winning performer, who has captivated audiences across six continents of our globe. Although emphasizing the history, struggles, and triumphs of the African American experience as well as African and southern folktales, Ferlatte also loves to tell stories that hold truths touching upon our common humanity, including personal stories as well as many tales from other cultures. She believes that telling and listening to one another's stories not only enables us to learn about and understand each other better. She views storytelling as a traditional art form that can promote literacy, imagination, and values in the young.

In addition to being nominated for a Grammy, Ferlatte's other awards include the National Storytelling Network's ORACLE Circle of Excellence Award, the National Association of Black Storytellers' Zora Neale Hurston Award, the California Arts Council's Highest Ranking, as well as many awards for her recordings.

5

Voices Beyond Boundaries: A Deeper Understanding

When the Story Is Ended: Storytelling for Community-Building

By Charles Temple

A hundred years ago, Alexander Carmichael attended a *cèilidh* on an Outer Hebrides island. Villagers of all ages crammed into a small cottage, and were spellbound by a tale spun out by a seasoned teller:

> *The tale is full of incident, action and pathos. It is told simply yet graphically, and at times dramatically—compelling the undivided attention of the listener.... Truth overcomes craft, skill conquers strength, and bravery is rewarded....* When the story is ended it is discussed and commented upon, and the different characters praised or blamed according to their merits and the views of the critics *[Emphasis added].—(Briggs, 1970)*

That last sentence is our focus here. These days when storytelling so strongly emphasizes performance, it is easy to forget that in all the years before our time, storytelling was a more participatory event: members of the audience were invited to create their own interpretations of what they heard and compare their views with those of diverse others. They not only listened to stories; they made meaning together. That's a good way to form trust among diverse people and build communities. I've learned to use those after-story discussions powerfully and fruitfully in the past 20 years working as a storytelling teacher in democratization and literacy projects in dozens of

---

countries around the world. In this article, I will share some techniques my team has used for creating discussions that follow good stories.

Stories that Invite Thinking and Sharing

Some stories pose their own questions

"The Cow-Tail Switch" from West Africa, and "The Theft of Smell" from Peru, are good examples. You can ask for predictions about how the stories will end, or you can use a fancier strategy such as Corners (see below) that gives people group support as they think of reasons to support their answers.

Some stories contain moral dilemmas that invite exploration

The stories may not come right out and ask a question, but the questions aren't hard to find. "The Seal's Skin" from Scotland and Iceland, and "The Happy Man's Shirt" from Italy (the Russian version from Tolstoy is "The King and the Shirt") are stories that can invite listeners to voice their own questions. But there are strategies that can deepen the discussion and lead to debate about issues raised by the story. Some of those strategies are Academic Controversy and the Value Line.

Some stories seem straightforward but can still yield up engaging issues with a little work

"Jack and the Beanstalk" from England; "Hansel and Gretel" from Germany; "The Boy Who Lived with the Bears" from the Seneca Indians of Upstate New York; "The Girl in the Drum" from Tanzania; and "A Gift of Laurel Blooms" from the Appalachian Mountains of Kentucky can all inspire interesting thoughts. But sometimes to get at the heart of things you need to twist them around or climb inside the skins of the characters and see what they are going through. Strategies like retelling them by casting people in different Dramatic Roles, or using the Audience Directs strategy can all lead to rich thoughts.

What Strategies?

Corners

Use Corners (Crawford, et al., 2005) after people have heard a story, to invite them to choose and defend different positions on an issue raised in that story. For Corners you need a story that poses a question with three or four defensible responses. (If the story doesn't have that many, get another story or another discussion strategy).

After choosing the question and teasing out some likely responses, explain to the participants that they are going to think about a question, stake out a position on it, and be ready to support their position.

Once you put the question and several possible answers to the group, have the participants order the answers from the most to least preferred. (Alternatively, you can have the participants count off by number, and assign them to corners. This strategy is recommended if you think the groups will not divide themselves evenly).

Next, have all of the participants who preferred the first response go to one corner, all those in favor of the second go to another corner, and so on. One corner can be for those who are undecided.

Now have the people in each corner share their views with each other. What are their reasons for taking the position they have chosen?

Invite representatives from the corners, one at a time, to state that group's position and the reasons the group has for supporting their views. Then welcome people from all groups to say what they think. Encourage them to politely (!) question and debate each other's ideas.

Explain now that some people may have had their minds changed by what they heard. If so, they should feel free to change groups by walking to the group they now agree with. (You can model this by walking dramatically from one group to another as you hear strong arguments!).

Finally, once the discussion has ended and everyone has moved to their final group, ask each group to summarize its position and the reasons that support it.

Debrief by asking the participants what they learned from the exercise.

Academic Controversy

Academic Controversy (Kagan, 1998) helps people practice the art of thinking critically—taking a position and producing reasons to support their arguments. It can also help them practice debating politely using arguments and reasons.

Assign people to groups of four and give them a binary question to discuss—one with a "yes" or "no," "this" or "that" answer, so people can take either of two sides to it.

People should begin by discussing the question in their groups of four, just so they reach a common understanding of what the question means and why it matters.

Then you have people count off within their group: 1, 2, 3, and 4 (if there are five people in any group, then there will be two with the number 1). Tell those with numbers 1 and 2 that they should prepare to argue for the point of view that says "Yes, we should." Tell numbers 3 and 4 that they should prepare to argue the point of view, "No, we shouldn't"—or however the issue divides.

Now direct both pairs within each group to go off by themselves, taking paper and pens with them, and have them spend a few minutes listing reasons to support their position.

Next, have each of the people with a "Yes" answer find a new partner with a "Yes" answer, sit with that new partner, exchange reasons for their answers, and write down any they did not already have on their lists. Those with a "No" answer should do the same.

Now have people return to their original partners and pool the reasons they learned from their new partners, together with the reasons they already had. Then they should think carefully about all of the reasons listed, think of the ones that best support their position, and prepare to debate the other pair within their group of four. To begin the debate, they should come up with a statement of their position, and two or three good reasons for it.

After a few more minutes, tell the pairs to join the other pairs in their group and begin the debate. One side states its position with the reasons for it, and the other does the same. Then they debate each other's arguments.

Let the debate go on for a bit—then tell everyone that they are now free to drop their assigned positions and express whatever opinions they personally believe. (Usually a collective sigh of relief goes up at this point!) Invite groups to come up with a consensus position: that is, a position with which everyone agrees, and also reasons to support it.

Finally, you can call on a member of each group to give a statement of the group's conclusions from their debate.

Value Line

The Value Line (Crawford, et al, op. cit.) is well suited for questions that have more than two good answers.

Pose a question to people on which answers may vary along a continuum. For example, after telling "Jack and the Beanstalk," you might ask, "Do you think we should consider Jack a hero?"

Give people a few minutes to consider the question alone and formulate answers, then stand on one side of the room and announce that you represent one pole, or extreme position, on the argument. You might say, "Yes, Jack was an outstanding hero. He defeated his enemy and got what he wanted." Invite a person to stand at the other end of the room to represent the opposite pole of the argument. The person might say, "No, I don't think Jack is a hero. We should never try to be like Jack. We would be terrible people if we behaved as he did."

Invite everyone else to line up between the two of you in places along the imaginary line between the two poles of the argument. Each stands at a point in the line that reflects his or her position on the question. Remind people to compare their views with those of people immediately around them to make sure they are all standing in the right spots. After hearing others' answers, some people might elect to move one way or another along the value line.

Identify three or four clusters of people who seem to represent different views on the question. Invite them to prepare a statement of their position and to share it with the whole group. Ask them to try to persuade others to move to their position. Afterward, discuss as a group what they learned from the exercise. What ideas and values came to light? (And did they note how we use geographical terms when we talk about "positions," "left" and "right" and "polarized" arguments?)

Following Dramatic Roles

As French drama critic Etienne Souriau pointed out many years ago (Souriau, 1955), we tend to understand characters in stories by the roles they play in the plot. That may be because, whether we are watching a sporting event or reading fiction, it is normal for us to cheer the hero, boo the rival, and make a warm place in our hearts for the trusty helper. Authors and storytellers wittingly or unwittingly use these propensities to shape the audience's reactions to characters: assigning one the role of protagonist or main character, another the role of helper, and another the role of rival or enemy.

The roles may be represented by their Zodiac symbols:

- ♌ *The Hero* is the character whose desire and need drives the story forward.
- ☼ *The Goal* is the hero's main need or object of desire.
- ♂ *The Rival* is the person or force that stands between the hero and her or his goal.
- ☾ *The Helper* is a person or force in a story that helps the hero achieve his or her goal.

You can use dramatic roles in several ways to think about stories. One way is to nominate candidates for each of the roles and discuss your choices.

These discussions can become lively, because not all role assignments are clear. Is the helper in "Jack and the Beanstalk" the mysterious old man or the giant's wife? If the helper is the giant's wife (and the giant is the rival), why should she help the person who is striving against her husband? Is Jack's goal to obey his mother, to satisfy his curiosity, to get wealth, or to prove himself? Or is it all of these things? Discussing these issues takes people below the surface of a story.

Another way of using dramatic roles is to take different perspectives on a story. Choose a character who seems to be playing one role and think how the story would be told if that character were playing a different role. For example, in "Jack and the Beanstalk," suppose the giant's wife were the hero; that is, suppose we saw things from her perspective. What is her goal? Who is her rival? Why did she help Jack? (And—hey—whatever happened to her, and why didn't we wonder before?!) Is the giant's wife like some women we know in our own communities? Exploring such questions can make even seemingly transparent stories explode with new meaning.

The Audience Directs

This is a dramatic activity (from Dorothy Heathcote's work, reported in Wagner, 1999) can yield fascinating insights. Begin by telling the story well. Immerse your audience in it with all of your skill as a storyteller.

Next, choose a critical moment to dramatize—preferably a turning point or points when the most is at stake. In "Jack and the Beanstalk," such a scene might be when Jack first approaches the giant's castle, knocks on the door, and is greeted by the giant's wife. In "The Girl in the Drum," it may be the moment when the misbehaving girl is rescued from the drum, in front of her parents, her well-behaved sisters, and their neighbors.

Recruit members of the audience to take each of the key roles. Explain to the audience that we must fully understand what is at stake for each character at this moment—what must be going through his mind—so she or he can act out the scene appropriately. Then have the characters stand in front of the group. Regarding Jack, you might ask, for example, what must be on his mind as he approaches the huge door? How large is the door in proportion to Jack? What makes him pound his fist on the door? What is at stake for him? What are his choices? What will he do if he *doesn't* knock on the door? Why does he decide to do it? Do the same for the giant's wife. How does the knocking sound to her—thunderous or puny? What does she think when she sees the small but plucky boy below her at her feet? What thoughts go through her mind, knowing what she knows about her husband? What are her feelings as she looks down at Jack? Ask the actors to focus their minds on a few of these considerations as they prepare to act out the scene.

- Dramatize the scene, using minimal props or none at all to help characters think their way into their roles. Ask the audience to watch carefully and see what the actors make them think of.
- After the drama is over, invite reflection. Ask the audience what they saw. Ask the actors what they thought about as they acted. What tensions did they feel, and what motives drove them?
- This activity, like the others mentioned in this article, can yield rich insights that go far beyond the story alone, and allow the audience to understand and appreciate other people's reasoning. Such activity goes a long way toward building communities.

- Whether they be entertainers, teachers, religious workers, or counselors, storytellers who follow a good story with discussions such as these reward their audiences with opportunities to participate in the story and midwife surprisingly rich insights. They invite people from different backgrounds to hear and understand each other. The skills of reasoning and the habit of open-mindedness and mutual understanding that come from good discussions can carry over into our lives, too: into our families, our lives in the workplace, our relations with our neighbors, and our choices as citizens and as voters.

References

Briggs, Katherine. *British Folk Tales.* New York: Pantheon, 1970.

Crawford, Alan, Wendy Saul, and Sam Mathews. *The Thinking Classroom.* New York and Budapest: Central European University Press, 2005.

Kagan, Spencer. *Cooperative Learning Strategies.* San Juan Capistrano, CA: Kagan Cooperative Learning, 1998.

Martinez, Miriam, Junko Yokota, and Charles Temple. *Teaching with Literature.* Lanham, MD: Rowman and Littlefield, 2017.

Souriau, Ettienne. *Les deux cent milles situations dramatiques.* Paris: Flamarion, 1955.

Wagner, Betty Jane. *Dorothy Heathcote: Drama as a learning medium.* Portsmouth, N.H.: Heinemann, 1999.

Sources of Stories

"The Cow-Tail Switch" is found in Harold Courlander and George Herzog, *The Cow-Tail Switch: And Other West African Stories.* New York: Square Fish, 2008. It is available online at westafrikanoralliterature.weebly.com/the-cow-tail-switch.html.

"The Boy Who Lived with the Bears" is from Joseph Bruchac, *The Boy Who Lived with the Bears: And Other Iroquois Stories.* Parabola, 2003. It is available online at www.firstpeople.us/FP-Html-Legends/TheBoyWhoLivedWithBears-Iroquois.html.

"The Seal's Skin" is available from several sources, including Jane Yolen's *Favorite Folk Tales from Around the World* (Pantheon, 1988), and Duncan Williamson's *Tales of the Seal People* (Interlink Publishing Group, 1998).

"The Girl in the Drum" was published in Tanzania by the International Book Bank in 2012. An electronic version is available by emailing Dr. Temple at Temple@hws.edu.

"The Theft of Smell" is available online at www.marilynkinsella.org/Fabulous%20Folktales/theft_of_smell.htm.

"A Gift of Laurel Blooms" is from Marie Campbell's *Tales from the Cloud Walking Country.* University of Georgia Press, 2000.

"The Happy Man's Shirt" is an Italian variation of Leo Tolstoy's fable "The King and the Shirt," online at https://fairietale.livejournal.com/11044.html.

Courtesy of Kevin Colton, chief photographer at Hobart and William Smith Colleges, Geneva, New York. Used by permission.

CHARLIE TEMPLE teaches storytelling, international education, literacy methods, and children's literature at Hobart and William Smith Colleges in Geneva, New York, USA, and works overseas for the Open Society Institute, USAID, CODE Canada, and the World Bank. He is a member of the Tejas Storytelling Association and serves on the board of directors of Storytelling in Higher Education (SHE) for the National Storytelling Network.

Epilogue: Where Do We Go from Here?

Heather Forest

After a story is over, it lingers. An oral tale, spoken or read out loud, sets listeners' imaginal world in motion, bringing memory and imagination into a vibrant synergy. People bring their own lived experience to the creative act of listening to a story and so each listener understands stories uniquely. A story, like a "thought seed," can take root in the heart and mind, grow, blossom, and bear fruit over time. A story can nourish its listeners as it gives rise to new realization. Cultures around the world have long used both realistic and nonrealistic folkloric tales in the shape of fables, epics, wonder tales, wisdom tales, and legends as tried-and-true teaching tools. As metaphor, folkloric stories offer insights into lived experience. Whether the hero or shero in a story is wise or foolish, listeners can vicariously learn from the choices the characters make as the plot unfolds. By bearing witness to the consequences of characters' choices in stories, listeners throughout history have indirectly learned how to make choices along their own life's journey. Perhaps this is why folktales, traveling far and wide, have been valued for their practical educational uses and been saved.

Historically, people around the globe migrated from one place to another as a result of social, political, economic, or environmental upheaval. Stories are light. They can be safely held in the heart instead of the hand and be transported as invisible cultural heirlooms from one territory to another. Folkloric tales that have been carried and preserved by oral tradition are treasured as "true," not because they "happened," but because there is a bit of "truth" in them. Folk stories are perpetuated to protect that priceless kernel of truth. Migrating from mouth to ear, passed on by being spoken again, or written as text and then read out loud, folk stories stitch in and out of the oral and literary tradition. Since ancient times, folktales have been powerful educational vessels for passing on wisdom, culture, and the worldview of their bearers. Wise, heroic characters model safe, socially effective choices. Cautionary tales featuring characters who make dangerous, selfish, or socially destructive choices offer guidance about how *not* to behave. The hero's choices, both wise and foolish, can reflect deeply held values of a culture and can shape and influence acceptable behavior in a community.

This carefully curated collection of folkloric tales is presented by storytellers who have a personal connection to the culture of the story they have contributed. To deepen readers' appreciation for the plot, each storyteller has written a short essay giving cultural context for their story, and each has crafted some relevant questions to ponder. This book offers a portal into many diverse cultures and models a way for educators to present folkloric tales to their students with the goal of stretching cultural horizons. These stories invite further investigation. Folktales, unlike fiction, are oral narratives that do not have a singular, identifiable author. Expanded and shaped by the tongues of tellers over time, polished and passed down from one generation to the next, folktales reflect the values and customs of the culture from which they come. Because folktale plots are generally concerned with life's universal themes, they can also transcend their culture of origin to reveal the commonality of human experience. This ancient form of narrative communication, for both education and entertainment, not only offers a window into culture, but also can be a mirror reflecting the comedy and pathos of our own lives. Studying folktales can encourage empathy, multicultural understanding, interpersonal dialogue on issues brought up by the stories, and can provide an opportunity to reflect. Studying the world's ancient folktales allows contemporary people to experience diverse cultures that thrived long ago, and to gain insight into present-day descendants of those cultures. Because folktales illuminate universal life experience, they can offer enlightening insights into traditions and values. Lessons taught through stories are easier to remember than a list of disconnected facts. As metaphor, folkloric stories can help young listeners utilize the wisdom of the ancients to make sense of our chaotic contemporary world.

Follow-Through Activities

After reading or hearing the stories in this book read out loud, students could explore the following.

Cartography

Have students locate on a world map the country or region from which a story in this book originates. Research the topography and ecology of the setting. Are any natural features of the environment reflected in the plot? After learning about the geographical setting of the story, ask students to describe how they imagined the "place" of the tale when they first heard it. Ask students to consider how a listener's lived experience affects how a story is imagined? Did all listeners imagine the same environmental details?

Geographic/Historical Transportation of a Folktale

Have students place a tale selected from this book in a time frame of history: preindustrial, ancient world, modern times, mythical time, etc. Has the tale traveled in any type of diaspora? If so, in which culture can the earliest version be found?

Science

How does the natural environment of a selected tale's setting affect the story? If animals are included, are the animals accurately or metaphorically depicted? Does the terrain contribute to the action?

Choices

Travel through the stories in this book and notice the points in the plots when characters make choices. Notice the resulting consequences. Ask students to consider if they have ever had to make similar choices in their own lives. Dialogue with students about choices made.

Universality

Ask students to identify challenges or ethical issues raised in a selected folktale. Ask them to make text-to-self connections, reflecting upon what happened in their own lives if or when they encountered similar challenges. Encourage the sharing of personal stories that link to those challenges or issues. In addition, identifying text-to-text and text-to-world connections will help students recognize universality in the stories.

Visual Arts

Have students create:

- A painting or drawing of a poignant moment of a selected folktale from this book
- A picture book based on the folktale
- A story mural

Drama/Literature

Have students create:

- A play based on a folktale plot from this book
- A radio show based on the plot
- A ballad or rap song that retells the plot
- A puppet show that retells the plot

Math and Patterns

Ask students to create a graphic time line or flowchart of events in a folktale plot selected from this book. Investigate conceptual structures in the plot: equations or balancing elements, cause-and-effect situations, logical sequences, possibilities, patterns, etc.

Societal Elements

Ask students to research any housing, tools, or attire described or mentioned in a folktale from this book. Ask students to research any aspects of daily life or religious customs reflected by the folktale. Ask students to consider how the lifestyles of characters in the folktale are similar or different from their own.

398.2

Based on the Dewey decimal system, school and public libraries shelve books of folktales in the 398.2 section of the library. This is part of the nonfiction section of the library because the study of folktales is part of cultural and social studies, akin to anthropology and archaeology. Ask students to find a folktale from their own family's cultural heritage and examine the tale. Have students share it with others as part of a classroom multicultural storytelling festival.

Conclusion

This book, utilizing storytelling as a portal to diverse cultures, offers educators an authentic glimpse into the cultural background of each tale. By expanding students' cultural horizons to encounter and appreciate unique differences between cultural heritages, a commonality of human experience may emerge. Nurture this awakening. Empathy is a path to peace.

We all share the same sky.

 HEATHER FOREST, PhD, is a modern-day bard. Her storytelling performances are a fusion of poetry, prose, original melody, and the sung and spoken word. A pioneer in the American storytelling revival, she has shared her repertoire of world tales in theaters, schools, literature conferences, and storytelling festivals throughout the United States and abroad. A multiple award-winning author and recording artist, she has published seven children's picture books based on folktales, three folktale anthologies, eight audio recordings of storytelling, and a popular educational website Story Arts Online, www.storyarts.org. Ms. Forest is a recipient of the Circle of Excellence Award presented by the National Storytelling Network, USA. Contact heather@storyarts.org.

Index

About the Editors

SHERRY NORFOLK is an award-winning storyteller, author, and teaching artist, performing and leading residencies and professional development workshops nationally and internationally. She has appeared in the Manitoba International Storytelling Festival, Taiwan International Storytelling Carnival, International Art of Storytelling Festival (Miami, Florida), International Storytelling Center (Jonesborough, Tennessee), Singapore International Storytelling Festival, Manila International Storytelling Festival, and many more festivals, schools, libraries, museums, and universities nationwide.

Sherry is a Kennedy Center Teaching Artist, a Wolf Trap Teaching Artist, an Arts Integration Teaching Artist with Tennessee Arts Commission's Value Plus Schools and Arts360 programs, and is on the rosters of the Mississippi Arts Commission, Louisiana State Arts Council, South Carolina Arts Commission, Virginia Commission for the Arts, and Springboard to Learning (Young Audiences) in St. Louis. She leads residencies in pre–K through high school classrooms across the country and Southeast Asia. An adjunct professor at Lesley University, Sherry is a recognized leader in integrating learning through storytelling.

She is coeditor and/or coauthor with Lyn Ford and Jane Stenson of books that explore rigorous, standards-based storytelling strategies for learning across the curriculum, including *Storytelling Strategies for Reaching and Teaching Children with Special Needs* (Libraries Unlimited, 2017). For more, see www.sherrynorfolk.com.

LYNETTE (LYN) FORD is a fourth-generation, nationally recognized Affrilachian storyteller and Ohio teaching artist who has shared programs and workshops on telling and writing stories with folks of all ages for more than 25 years. Lyn's storytelling has made her a featured teller, keynote speaker, and workshop presenter in venues across the country and from Australia to Ireland. Lyn's work is published in several storytelling-in-education resources, as well as in her award-winning books: *Affrilachian Tales: Folktales from the African-American Appalachian Tradition;*

Beyond the Briar Patch: Affrilachian Folktales, Food and Folklore; Hot Wind, Boiling Rain: Scary Stories for Strong Hearts (2017 Storytelling World Award winner and a creative-writing resource); and *Boo-Tickle Tales: Not-So-Scary Stories for Ages 4 to 9,* written with storytelling friend and fellow teaching artist, Sherry Norfolk. Lyn is also a Certified Laughter Yoga Teacher, and a great-grandmother. For more, see www.storytellerlynford.com